Date Due

SEP. 20 1994	APR. 23 1996
OCT. 3 1994	9 JAN 1997
FEB. 2 1995	4 FEB 1997
MAR. 16 1995	30 APR 1997
APR. 12 1995	14 OCT 1998
APR. 27 1995	
22	26 MAY 1999
MAY 18 1995	11 NOV 1999
OCT. 10 1995	23 FEB 2000
OCT. 26 1995	
NOV. 7 1995	
DEC. 1 1995	25 OCT 2000
	13 MAR 2001
DEC. 20 1995	17 DEC 2001
JAN. 24 1996	
FEB. 6 1996	
MAR. 14 1996	16 APR 2001

AMERICA the BEAUTIFUL

HAWAI'I

By Sylvia McNair

Consultants

Dorothy Hazama, Ph.D., College of Education, University of Hawaii

Neil J. Hannahs, Director, Public Affairs Department, Kamehameha Schools

Robert L. Hillerich, Ph.D., Bowling Green State University, Bowling Green, Ohio

CHILDRENS PRESS®
CHICAGO

Lanikai Beach, O'ahu

Project Editor: Joan Downing
Associate Editor: Shari Joffe
Design Director: Margrit Fiddle
Typesetting: Graphic Connections, Inc.
Engraving: Liberty Photoengraving

Library of Congress Cataloging-in-Publication Data

McNair, Sylvia.
    America the beautiful. Hawaii / by Sylvia McNair.

        p.   cm.
    Includes index.
    Summary: Describes the geography, people, history,
tourism, government, and culture of the youngest of the
fifty states.
    ISBN 0-516-00457-3
    1.   Hawaii—Juvenile literature.
[1.   Hawaii.]   I.   Title.
DU623.25.M39   1989   89-35084
996.9—dc20   CIP
                                                       AC

The Royal Hawaiian Hotel in Waikīkī

TABLE OF CONTENTS

Chapter 1

THE *ALOHA* SPIRIT

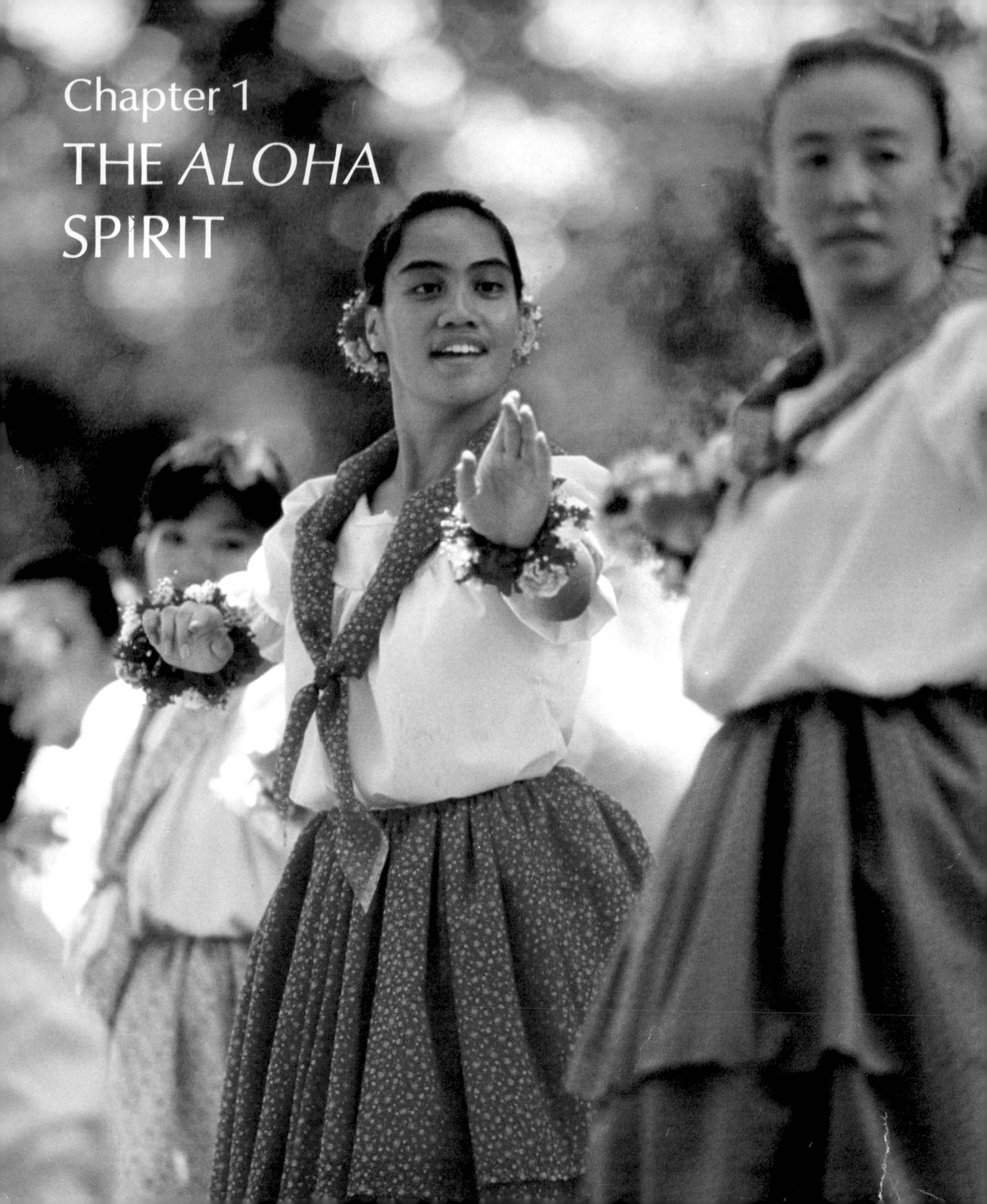

THE *ALOHA* SPIRIT

Aloha is a Hawaiian word understood by everyone. It means "hello," "love," "goodbye," and more. It is always a warm greeting, implying friendship and said with a smile. Translated literally, it is the combination of *alo*, "to face"; and *ha*, "the breath of life."

The *Aloha* spirit is what sets Hawai'i apart from all other places. Hawai'i is the youngest of the fifty United States, both geologically and politically. The last one to be admitted to the Union, it is unique in many ways. It is the only state that was once a kingdom. It is the only state first explored and inhabited by Polynesians from the South Pacific. It is the only state that lies in the tropics, with balmy temperatures at its seacoasts year-round. It is the only state formed entirely by volcanoes.

Hawai'i's beautiful beaches, towering mountains, and brilliant tropical plants are familiar to the entire world through movies, postcards, and tourism posters.

But the islands' biggest boosters will tell you that the most outstanding and unusual characteristic of the state is the friendly welcome extended to outsiders. People of many races and national backgrounds have come to Hawai'i's shores, fallen in love with its beauty and way of life, and decided to live there. Visitors are greeted with flower *leis* and sweet music; their memories of the islands' soft tropical beauty bring them back again and again.

Chapter 2
THE LAND

THE LAND

White sands, blue seas, and the red fire of volcanoes—the colors of Hawai'i are those of the American flag. Visitors to the islands are struck by these and other vivid splashes of color. Trees are ablaze with coral, flame-red, lavender, and gold-colored blossoms. Fields are carpeted with purple orchids, bright green sugarcane, pink bougainvillea blossoms, and orange bird of paradise. Islanders and visitors alike dress in loose shirts and dresses that copy the brilliant hues of nature.

Hawai'i is made up of a string of islands in the North Pacific Ocean more than 2,000 miles (3,219 kilometers) southwest of California. The entire chain, which is some 1,523 miles (2,451 kilometers) long, includes 132 islands.

The state of Hawai'i includes eight major islands. Starting in the west, they are Ni'ihau, Kaua'i, O'ahu, Moloka'i, Lāna'i, Maui, Kaho'olawe, and Hawai'i. The island of Hawai'i is sometimes called the Big Island to distinguish the island from the state. The 124 minor islands, most of which are small, unpopulated atolls (coral reefs surrounding lagoons) in the northwest portion of the island chain, are administered by the United States Department of the Interior.

Hawai'i is a small state. Its eight major islands cover a total of 6,471 square miles (16,760 square kilometers). In area, Hawai'i ranks forty-seventh among the fifty states; only Rhode Island, Delaware, and Connecticut are smaller.

Lava flow during an eruption of Mauna Loa

Hawai'i is actually one long, partially submerged mountain range rising up from the floor of the ocean. It was created by the eruption of volcanoes, a process that started millions of years ago and still continues. Two volcanoes on the Big Island, Mauna Loa and Kīlauea, are still active. Kīlauea erupts quite frequently, creating huge displays of fireworks as fountains of burning lava spout upward. Three sister volcanoes, Mauna Kea and Hualālai on the Big Island and Haleakalā on neighboring Maui, have been quiet for a long time and are classified as dormant. Dormant does not mean dead, however, and geologists and volcanologists (scientists who study volcanoes) believe that any of those three could become active again at some time in the future.

Hawai'i is the largest of the eight main islands, followed in size by Maui, O'ahu, Kaua'i, Moloka'i, Lāna'i, Ni'ihau, and Kaho'olawe. Measured in geological terms, the Hawaiian Islands are comparatively young land masses. The earth's major continents were well established some 300 million years ago. In contrast, the mountain peaks of the Hawaiian Islands began to push above sea level only within the last 25 million years, making them among the newest places on earth.

The eight main islands of Hawai'i have a common culture and history. They are also similar in geography, with high, severely eroded inland mountains that slope down to the seashores. Two Hawaiian words are used frequently on all the islands to indicate direction: *mauka*, meaning "toward the mountains," and *makai*, meaning "toward the sea."

KAUA'I

Kaua'i is called the Garden Isle, for two reasons. It has some of the most luxurious natural vegetation in the state, and it has four outstanding botanic gardens.

The island is nearly circular in shape, with Mount Wai'ale'ale rising in the center. About 500 inches (1,270 centimeters) of rain fall each year on the eastern slope of this mountain, making it the rainiest spot in the world. A view of the mountain from a distance shows dark strips leading down its sides. They are thin canyons, carved over many centuries by fierce torrents of rain cascading down the mountainside.

The northwest coast of the island, called Nā Pali (meaning "the

Abundant rainfall has produced especially luxurious vegetation on the island of Kaua'i.

cliffs''), is covered with rugged cliffs that lead straight down to the sea. No roads have been built along this stretch. Dramatic Waimea Canyon cuts a deep gorge west of Mount Wai'ale'ale; its spires and other rock formations resemble those in Arizona's Grand Canyon.

The heavy rainfall has given Kaua'i even richer vegetation than that on the other Hawaiian islands. Giant tree ferns grow in the rain forests. Rare plants and birds that exist nowhere else on earth flourish here, although many of them are endangered species.

Alaka'i Swamp, in the heart of the island, is a dense jungle with a few tea-colored streams and black mud bogs that are hazardous for hikers. Waterfalls tumble from the swampland to green, fertile valleys below. There are hot, dry spots on Kaua'i, too, as well as some of the state's most beautiful beaches.

Kaua'i has been attacked more than once by huge, destructive tidal waves that have flooded its shores and wiped out entire villages.

NI'IHAU

About 17 miles (27 kilometers) west of Kaua'i, across a channel, is Ni'ihau, sometimes called the Forbidden Island. The entire island is a privately owned cattle and sheep ranch, and few outsiders are allowed to visit. Its climate is dry; precipitation becomes trapped in the mountains of Kaua'i and rain seldom falls on Ni'ihau. Low plains lie at each end of the 18-mile- (29-kilometer-) long island, and a high tableland lies in the middle. Lake Hālāli'i, in the center of the island, is the largest natural lake in the state.

O'AHU

O'ahu, the island of the city of Honolulu, is home of such world-famous landmarks as Waikīkī Beach, Diamond Head, and Pearl Harbor. The island is aptly called the Gathering Place, since 80 percent of the state's people live there. The entire island, with about three-quarters of a million residents, is part of the county of Honolulu.

Two mountain ranges, the Ko'olau and the Wai'anae, stretch in a northwesterly direction from the beaches and harbors in the south. If you are in a high-rise building in the heart of the city in the evening and look toward the north, you'll see that the bright city lights come to an abrupt stop at the edge of the mountains. In between the two mountain ranges is a fertile plain where pineapples are grown. Sugarcane fields are found near the coast.

The Koʻolau Mountain Range runs along the eastern side of Oʻahu.

Often, it is raining on the mountaintops while the sun is shining brightly at the beaches. Giant waves crash along Oʻahu's northwest coast, making it a popular spot for surfing.

MOLOKAʻI

Molokaʻi, known as the Friendly Isle, was formed by three separate volcanoes. A flat stretch of land in the center of the northern coast is separated from the rest of the island by high cliffs. Sandy beaches lie on the west end of the long island. In the center are fertile agricultural fields. The eastern third is covered with high mountains and deep canyons.

Livestock is raised on the fertile plains of western Moloka'i.

At one time, man-made fish ponds could be found along the coasts of all the islands. Ancient Hawaiians constructed these ponds by building stone walls in shallow, offshore areas and at the mouths of natural inlets. Wooden gratings allowed small fish to enter and prevented large fish from leaving. The ponds were built to provide plenty of fish for Hawai'i's early chiefs. The southern coast of Moloka'i contains the state's largest concentration of ruins of these fish ponds.

LĀNA'I

Lāna'i, called the Pineapple Island because most of it is a commercially owned pineapple plantation, has one extinct volcanic crater, Pālāwai. During the summer harvest season, more than a million pineapples a day are taken from this island.

The Garden of the Gods, a dry area of strangely shaped lava formations and boulders, lies near Lāna'i City.

On the island of Lāna'i is an area of strangely shaped lava formations known as the Garden of the Gods.

MAUI

Maui is an unusually shaped island. Like the other Hawaiian islands, it consists of mountains that slope steeply down to the coast. However, Maui looks as if it were two islands that got stuck together as cookies sometimes do while they are baking.

The western part of the island, roughly circular in shape, is dominated by 'Eke Crater and the West Maui Mountains. In the east are Haleakalā Crater and Hanakauhi Mountain. The valley between—which gives the island its nickname, the Valley Isle—is a fertile area of sugarcane and pineapple plantations.

The terrain at the northern end of West Maui and the southern end of East Maui is so rugged that there are stretches where only four-wheel-drive vehicles can get through. Almost all of the island's settlements are along the shore, and few roads reach into the mountainous interior.

The highest point on the island is the summit of Mount Haleakalā, which rises 10,023 feet (3,055 meters) above sea level.

Wai'ānapanapa State Park on the east coast of Maui

Haleakalā has the largest inactive volcanic crater in the world. All of Manhattan could fit inside Haleakalā Crater; it is 3,000 feet (914 meters) deep and measures 22 miles (35 kilometers) in circumference.

KAHO'OLAWE

Kaho'olawe, the smallest of the state's eight major islands, is uninhabited. A barren, windswept piece of land, it is used by the United States armed forces as a target-practice area.

In the past, the island has been used for ranching and as a penal colony. Ancient Hawaiian fishing families who once occupied Kaho'olawe left sites of ancient shrines.

HAWAI'I

The Big Island of Hawai'i is roughly three-sided. It stretches 93 miles (150 kilometers) from north to south and 76 miles (122 kilometers) from east to west. It is the only one of the islands that still has quite frequent volcanic activity.

As on the other islands, the land of the Big Island rises sharply from the seashore to the inland mountains. The Big Island's two huge peaks, 13,677-foot (4,169-meter) Mauna Loa and 13,796-foot (4,205-meter) Mauna Kea, are the highest points in the state. Some scientists say that these qualify as the highest mountains on earth. They point out that from the ocean floor, where these mountains actually begin, they rise more than 30,000 feet (9,144 meters), several hundred feet more than the height of Mount Everest.

On Hawai'i, people seek out, rather than avoid, volcanic eruptions. Most volcanoes erupt with great violence and little or no warning. They spurt forth like soda from a bottle that has been shaken up just before it is uncapped. The lava in the Hawaiian chain of volcanoes, however, is relatively thin and liquid and contains less gas than the lava in other types of volcanoes. It builds up gradually, finds a crack in the earth, shoots upward like a fountain, and then flows—rather gently—down the slopes in a broad, flame-red stream. Because the flow is slow, people have time to rush out to watch nature's fiery show from a safe distance.

Mauna Loa and its sister peak, Kīlauea, have both erupted intermittently ever since people have lived on the Hawaiian Islands. Hawai'i Volcanoes National Park includes both of them. Kīlauea is especially active, erupting nearly every year.

Mauna Kea is a dormant volcano. Its name means "White Mountain," and because it is so high, there is actually enough snow on its summit to allow skiing in the winter.

There is great variety in the land of the Big Island. Lush valleys and fields produce sugarcane, fruits, coffee, and macadamia nuts. In contrast, the island also includes desertlike stretches of lava, sand, and ash. Between the north coast and the summit of Mauna Kea is the 250,000-acre (101,173-hectare) Parker Ranch, one of the largest cattle spreads in the United States. A few of the island's beaches are deep, white sand, while others are made of crushed, black lava. The island even boasts an unusual green sand beach that is made of volcanic olivine particles.

LAKES AND RIVERS

Because the islands are quite small, there are no large lakes or rivers in Hawai'i. Wailuku River, on the Big Island, is the longest and largest river in the state.

The only large natural lake is Hālāli'i Lake, which lies on Ni'ihau and spreads over 182 acres (74 hectares). Two reservoirs are larger: Wahiawā on O'ahu and Waitā on Kaua'i.

CLIMATE

Hawai'i is a subtropical state, with pleasantly mild temperatures all year. In the 1860s, one resident wrote, "Our sun always shines, our trees are always green, our trade winds always blow, our atmosphere is always pure." Another person described Hawai'i as "never too hot, never too cold, and always too beautiful."

The temperature varies little from summer to winter and from day to night. Except in the mountains, which are nearly always cool, the temperature stays between 70 and 85 degrees Fahrenheit (21 and 29 degrees Celsius) most of the time. A record high of 100 degrees Fahrenheit (38 degrees Celsius) occurred at Pāhala on the

The Big Island, famous for
its black sand beaches (left),
even boasts an unusual green
sand beach (above).

island of Hawai'i in 1931. In 1961, an all-time low of 14 degrees
Fahrenheit (minus 10 degrees Celsius) was recorded at Haleakalā
Crater. Temperatures of less than 60 degrees Fahrenheit
(15 degrees Celsius) are rare near sea level.

Yearly rainfall varies from as much as 500 inches (1,270
centimeters) in the mountains and high forests of Kaua'i to as
little as 10 inches (25 centimeters) in some parts of the lowlands.
Trade winds drop the heaviest rainstorms over the mountains on
the northeastern sides of the islands.

Nature can be cruel sometimes, even in this paradise. Tidal
waves have occasionally wiped out large areas of beach property
and have caused considerable loss of life. The islands also
experience frequent minor earthquakes. Volcanoes, while not
usually a threat to people because there is almost always time to
get out of the path of flowing lava, do occasionally destroy
residential neighborhoods.

Chapter 3
THE PEOPLE

THE PEOPLE

THE FIRST HAWAIIANS

The first people to live on the remote coral and lava islands in the North Pacific known as Hawai'i came from Polynesia, a group of Pacific islands more than 2,000 miles (3,219 kilometers) to the south. These early Polynesian sailors, who are thought to have come from the Marquesas Islands, about A.D. 300, had amazing skill. They traveled, without the aid of any navigational instruments, in large, double-hulled canoes. They developed their knowledge of sea routes by observing the stars and following the migration routes of birds.

Primitive fishhooks and cutting tools found on the Hawaiian Islands have been identified, through radiocarbon dating, as having been used sometime between A.D. 500 and 800. This proves that the first courageous sailors arrived at least that long ago. Anthropologists believe that the next group of Polynesian settlers, who are thought to have come from Tahiti, arrived in Hawai'i about five hundred or six hundred years later.

When this second group arrived, they discovered that people were already living on the islands. Hawaiian legends tell of the *menehune*, a race of little people who lived on the islands and only worked at night. It is possible that these legends grew out of the Tahitian settlers' first encounters with the descendants of the original Polynesian settlers. Fearful of the newcomers, the people already on the islands may have tried to stay out of sight during daylight.

The native Hawaiians—the descendants of the two early Polynesian groups—prospered over the next several centuries. By the time British naval captain James Cook and other Europeans arrived in the late 1700s, more than a quarter of a million Hawaiians lived on the islands.

A LAND OF MANY CULTURES

Honolulu's skyline, with its tall hotels and office buildings, looks much like many other large American cities. However, as one travels around the islands, one begins to notice many differences between Hawai'i and the other forty-nine states.

Most obvious is the racial diversity of the state. Hawai'i is truly a crossroads between East and West. People from many countries have been attracted to these islands for more than two hundred years. Petite Asians, broad-shouldered Samoans and Hawaiians, tall blondes with fair skin, dark-skinned blacks, and many people with features that suggest a multiracial heritage all call Hawai'i their home. The number of people with a mixture of ethnic backgrounds is increasing, because today, about half the marriages that take place on the islands involve couples of different racial backgrounds.

Japan, China, Korea, the Philippines, Southeast Asia, Tahiti, Tonga, New Zealand, Samoa, the United States, and several European countries have contributed to the rich mix of cultures in Hawai'i. Foods, festivals, architecture, and languages reflect the diversity. Although English is used universally in Hawai'i, about a quarter of those over the age of five speak a language other than English at home.

It is sometimes said that everyone in Hawai'i is a member of an ethnic minority, since no single ethnic group constitutes more than about one third of the population. Less than 1 percent of the people in Hawai'i are of pure Hawaiian extraction, meaning that they are descended solely from the Polynesians who first settled Hawai'i. Another 18 percent are of mainly Hawaiian ancestry.

About one third of Hawai'i's residents are Caucasian. Asians make up nearly 40 percent of the total population: 23 percent are Japanese, 11 percent are Filipino, 4.5 percent are Chinese, and 1 percent are Korean. Two percent of Hawai'i's people are black, and Samoans and Puerto Ricans each represent less than 1 percent of the population.

Some of the whites born in Hawai'i are descended from one of three groups that began arriving in Hawai'i in the 1800s: American missionaries; Portuguese, English, French, and other European sailors who abandoned the sea when they saw the beauty of the islands; and planters and merchants who emigrated from the United States or Europe to seek their fortune in Hawai'i.

The earliest Asian immigrants in Hawai'i were Chinese. Even before 1800, a few Chinese sailors jumped ship to stay on the islands, just as some of the Portuguese crewmen were doing. During the next few decades, Chinese laborers were brought over under contracts to work on Hawaiian sugarcane plantations for five-year periods. Some stayed only long enough to work out their contracts; others carefully saved their tiny wages and opened small shops, in time becoming successful merchants.

Japanese immigrants first came to Hawai'i in 1868, with three-year contracts to work on the plantations. King Kalākaua, who reigned from 1874 to 1891, actively encouraged Japanese immigration.

In 1906, Filipino laborers were brought to Hawai'i to work on a sugar plantation on the Big Island. Over the next forty years, more than 125,000 Filipino laborers were brought to the islands, and in

Hawai'i's multiethnic society led one famous writer to call the islands the "meeting place of East and West."

time there were more Filipinos in Hawai'i than anywhere else outside of the Philippines.

HAWAI'I'S 'ŌLELO MAKUAHINE

Hawai'i has two official state languages: English and Hawaiian. The 'ōlelo makuahine (mother language) of the Hawaiian people has a beautiful, liquid sound.

Hawaiian was solely a spoken language before the first American missionaries came to Hawai'i in 1820. One of their first goals was to establish phonetic spellings of Hawaiian words so that the language could be written down. Twelve letters from the English alphabet are used to spell Hawaiian words—the five vowels plus seven consonants: H, K, L, M, N, P, and W.

Only a very few people, such as many of the residents of Ni'ihau, use Hawaiian as their primary language. But everybody in Hawai'i sprinkles their speech with Hawaiian words. *Mahalo* (thank you), *kāne* (man), and *wahine* (woman) are commonly used Hawaiian words. People who have lived in Hawai'i for a long time, whatever their ancestry or place of birth, are called

Hawai'i's religious diversity is reflected in such beautiful shrines as the Buddhist Byodo-In Temple (left) and the Mormon Temple (right), both on O'ahu.

kama'āina. The Hawaiian word for newcomer is *malihini*. *Haole* means foreigner, or non-Hawaiian. Today, it refers to Caucasians of European or American descent. So a Caucasian person who is a native of the islands, or a long-time resident, is both a *kama'āina* and a *haole*.

POPULATION DISTRIBUTION

According to the 1980 census, Hawai'i has 964,961 residents, making it thirty-ninth in population among the fifty states. Hawai'i's population increased by 25 percent between 1970 and 1980, a growth rate more than twice that of the United States as a whole. About four-fifths of the state's people live on O'ahu. The population density on that island is 1,235 residents per square mile (477 people per square kilometer), compared with only 149 people per square mile (58 people per square kilometer) statewide. By comparison, the population density of the United States as a whole is 67 people per square mile (26 people per square kilometer).

Tourism is so prevalent in Hawai'i that on an average day, there are more than one hundred visitors on the islands for every thousand residents; and during each year, four times as many people visit the islands as live there!

Unlike the people who live in such popular tourist centers as Honolulu, residents of the Forbidden Isle of Ni'ihau seldom see outsiders.

RELIGION

Hawai'i's ethnic diversity has produced a religious diversity as well. Early Protestant missionaries taught their beliefs to the native Hawaiians. Buddhism and Shinto faiths were introduced to the islands by Japanese immigrants. Small groups of residents follow Jewish, Hindu, or Muslim beliefs. Some people of Hawaiian descent continue to preserve the ancient religious traditions of their people.

Catholics make up the largest single religious group. About 20 percent of the state's people are Catholic, 11 percent belong to other Christian denominations, and 6 percent are Buddhist. The leading Protestant denomination is the Church of Jesus Christ of Latter-day Saints (also known as the Mormon church).

THE MILITARY

Hawai'i is not all tourist resorts and tropical plantations. In fact, one writer called the state a "sugar-coated fortress." Nearly a fifth of the state's population is made up of people who work for the United States military and their families. The Pacific Command, based on O'ahu, is the largest command force in the world. Four army posts, two air-force bases, two marine-corps bases, and two navy bases lie on O'ahu. These bases occupy one-fourth of the island's land.

Chapter 4
OUT OF A MISTY PAST

OUT OF A MISTY PAST

Hawai'i's ancient history is shrouded in mystery, but clues to that mystery are found in the *mele*, the songs and chants; and the *'ōlelo*, the oral tradition.

Men and women lived in various parts of the earth for millions of years before inventing the means of putting words on paper. The times that occurred before people were able to preserve their history through written records are called prehistoric times. All our knowledge of how prehistoric people lived—and what important events occurred that shaped the lives of future generations—is sketchy and incomplete.

Archaeologists find clues in the few tools, utensils, and pieces of artwork they find buried under the earth. Other clues come from stories that have been passed down from generation to generation.

Over hundreds of years, myths, legends, and facts become so interwoven that modern historians cannot say for certain where the legends leave off and history begins. But because many of the stories handed down in Hawai'i are so similar to those told back in Polynesia, we can be sure they contain at least some kernels of truth about the ancient islanders. The heroes of these stories were almost certainly actual people, even though their superhuman deeds became greatly exaggerated as time went on.

Ancient Polynesian society was organized into separate tribes, each headed by an *ali'i*, or chief. Chiefs inherited their titles and their lands. Some, quite powerful, were *ali'i nui*—high chiefs, or kings. An *ali'i nui* might rule over several lesser chiefs.

Athletic competitions, such as boxing matches, were very popular among the ancient Hawaiians.

After the Hawaiian Islands were settled by ancient Polynesians, one or several *ali'i nui* ruled each of the major islands. This high position, however, was not hereditary. When an *ali'i nui* died, the surviving *ali'i* competed for the throne. They demonstrated various feats of strength, skill, and cleverness to prove their superiority and worthiness to lead.

Athletic competitions were sometimes conducted for the purpose of selecting men who would act as close companions to the leaders. Riding surfboards over huge waves, tobogganing down the slopes of grassy hills, foot racing, canoeing, boxing, and javelin throwing were among the sporting events popular with the ancient islanders. Prehistoric Hawaiians did not use specific dates to describe when a particular historical event occurred. They kept track of important events through genealogies (family histories). Some of their chants were records of chiefly and

An eighteenth-century sketch of a double-hulled Hawaiian canoe

priestly families, and important events were marked in time as having occurred during the reign of a certain chief.

POLYNESIAN MYTHOLOGY AND LEGENDS

Hawaiian chiefs claimed to be descended from a Polynesian demigod (a human who possesses godlike power) named Māui. Like Atlas, the superpowerful man in Greek mythology, Māui was able to hold the heavens on his shoulders. In fact, he created space for people to live between the heavens and earth by pushing the sky high up in the air. Among other accomplishments, he discovered how to make fire, lassoed the sun and made it move more slowly across the sky, and fished the islands of Hawai'i and New Zealand out of the ocean with a magic hook.

Hawai'i-loa, a skilled Polynesian sailor, is another legendary hero. He is credited with having found and named the volcanic islands of Hawai'i. He sailed back to his home in Java and brought his family to live in the new land. Traditional chants tell of his travels through a many-colored ocean where the fishes swam and the sun reflected beautifully on the waves.

High priests (*kahuna*) were as important in the ancient
Polynesian and Hawaiian societies as chiefs. A man named Pa'ao,
from Samoa, is considered the founder of Hawai'i's high-priest
family. Sometime around A.D. 1100, Pa'ao and some friends
moved north to the Hawaiian Islands. Later, he sent messengers to
Tahiti to persuade Pili, a high chief, to join him. Many legends are
told about these two men. For the next eight hundred years, their
descendants were the high priests and chiefs of Hawai'i.

A ruler named La'a is believed to have traveled, as a child, from
Tahiti to Hawai'i and back again sometime during the thirteenth
century. He was traveling to visit his uncle Mo'i-keha, high chief
of Kaua'i. Similar Tahitian legends tell of a ruler named Ra'a,
whose descendants have continued as Tahitian chiefs into the
twentieth century. He is almost certainly the same man, since
confusion between "l" and "r" is common in translating from one
dialect to another.

Mo'i-keha sent one of his sons to Tahiti to beg La'a to come
back to his childhood home. The mission succeeded, and in
Hawai'i, La'a was presented with three wives. Each of the wives
produced a son, and the families who were descended from these
sons were prominent in Hawai'i for centuries, proudly calling
themselves the "children of La'a."

KAPU, RULES FOR EVERYDAY LIFE

The great Polynesian sailors who settled Hawai'i brought their
religious and social systems with them. Over the years, strict rules
developed that governed everyday life. Priests controlled matters
of religion; chiefs had the authority in civil affairs.

A caste system, somewhat like that of feudal Europe,
determined a person's social status. According to their ancestry,

people were either *ali'i* (chiefs or nobles), *kahuna* (priests, teachers, medicine men, or other wise men), or *maka'āinana* (commoners).

High priests and high chiefs held the highest rank. Below them were chiefs, who ruled over sections of land within the islands. They owed their allegiance to the high chief or chiefs who ruled their particular island. Common people were of a lesser rank and the chiefs had absolute authority over them. Commoners could, however, leave one chief to serve another. Similarly, chiefs could transfer their allegiance from one high chief to another, or from island to island, without losing chiefly status.

Polynesian Hawaiians believed in many gods, and they appealed to these gods for help in all their activities: fishing, building their homes, making things, battling their enemies.

There were four principal gods. Kū was the patron god of war. Kāne, ancestor of all chiefs and commoners, was lord of sunlight, fresh water, and the life substances in nature. Lono was god of peace, fertility, and agriculture. Kanaloa ruled over the ocean and was the patron god of healing.

The Hawaiians were a very spiritual people. They offered prayers and offerings of food to their gods before undertaking any task and after completing their work. Because they believed that all living things possessed *mana* (divine power), they respected nature. They conserved things in nature and took only what they needed.

At the heart of both social and religious life was a body of elaborate rules called *kapu*. The word *kapu* means ''forbidden.'' It comes from the same Polynesian word as the word *taboo*, a word that has become part of the English language.

Kapu established a system of laws for the *ali'i* and the *maka'āinana*. The *ali'i* were believed to be earthly representatives and relatives of the gods. One rule of *kapu* forbade a *maka'āinana* to

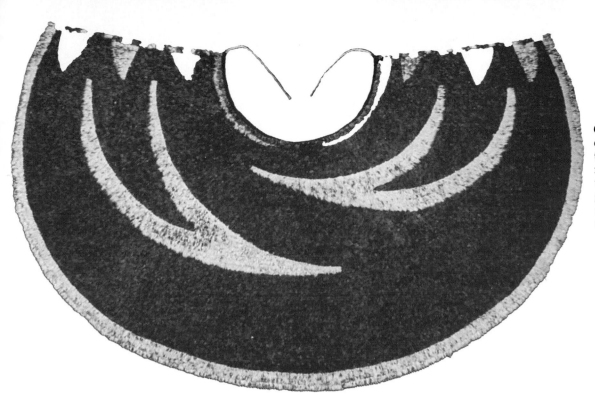

On special occasions, the highest-ranking chiefs wore exquisite garments made of thousands of feathers.

allow his shadow to fall across the path of a high *ali'i*. Another forbade men and women to eat together. Death by violent means was often the punishment for breaking *kapu*.

Some of the *kapu* laws were made by the chiefs and the *kahuna* solely for the purpose of maintaining order within the society. Other laws were based on logic, such as those designed to conserve natural resources.

INTERISLAND WARFARE

Religious ceremonies on the islands were ritualistic and colorful. Battles, too, followed certain ritualistic patterns. Warriors traveled in royal canoes that were fitted with triangular sails woven from dried leaves and had brilliant banners flying from the masts. As symbols of royalty, chiefs wore helmets, capes, and full-length cloaks made of thousands of brightly hued birds' feathers.

The feather cloaks were so elaborate that it could take as long as a hundred years to make one. Only the most prized feathers were used. Some were so tiny that fifty of them covered only the area of a person's fingernail. Yellow feathers were taken from a now-extinct bird called the *mamo*; only a few feathers from each bird were used. The finished cloaks had a deep, soft pile colored with some of nature's most splendid shades of yellow and crimson. The most famous, Kamehameha's cloak, has the feathers of more than eighty thousand *mamo* birds.

The commoners and chiefs wore clothes of tapa cloth, a material made from the inner bark of the paper mulberry tree. The sheets of paper cloth were pounded until they were soft and pliable, then dipped in or stamped with various dyes. Sometimes they were soaked in nut oils to make them waterproof.

In 1776, just as the American colonists were preparing to fight for their freedom from England, the high chiefs of Hawai'i's several islands were struggling against one another for superiority. The contest between the chiefs of Hawai'i and Maui was particularly bitter. Strategic battles were fought on Maui at about the same time as the Boston Tea Party and the Battle of Bunker Hill were taking place in Massachusetts.

After a sound defeat, the chief of Hawai'i agreed to peace terms and retreated to the Big Island, still planning revenge on Maui's chief. This was the state of political and military affairs in the islands when Captain James Cook arrived.

EAST AND WEST MEET IN HAWAI'I

The first person to write about Hawai'i in any detail was British Captain James Cook. In July 1776, Cook had set sail from England in search of a Northwest Passage to the Atlantic. During that same month, American colonists in Philadelphia, Pennsylvania, were signing a Declaration of Independence from England, the first step toward establishing a new nation that would eventually include Hawai'i.

Captain Cook landed on Kaua'i in January of 1778. Though he did not know it at the time, these islands marked the last significant pieces of land on earth to be found and documented by Western explorers. Since that time, maps and globes of the earth have been quite complete. There is evidence that Spanish seafarers visited the islands before Captain Cook, but they left no journals or other written accounts of their discoveries. Archives in Spain contain maps that show some islands called Los Majos, discovered in 1555 by a Spaniard named Juan Gaetano. These islands may, in fact, have been the Hawaiian Islands. However, during Captain Cook's time, the rest of the world knew nothing of this early discovery.

On the Hawaiian Islands, Captain Cook was astounded to find Polynesian settlements so distant from those he had visited in Polynesia. He named the islands the Sandwich Islands after his patron, the Earl of Sandwich. Although this was what the Western world called the islands for many years to come, the name was never accepted by the islands' inhabitants.

The native Hawaiians on Kaua'i greeted Cook with friendship and gifts of food and water. By coincidence, the foreign ships arrived during a festival honoring Lono, god of the harvest. The Hawaiians decided that these strange-looking, light-skinned people were gods, and they called Captain Cook "Lono." Cook's sailors were welcomed warmly by the islanders as well. After two weeks, the Englishmen said their goodbyes and sailed northward.

Seeking shelter during the winter, Cook returned to Hawai'i in January 1779, this time to the Big Island. Once again, he arrived

Believing Captain Cook to be a reincarnation of the god Lono, the people of the Big Island greeted him joyously with gifts of food and water.

during the season honoring the god Lono. He was greeted joyously as Lono, who had left long ago but had promised to return someday. After two weeks of celebration, Cook and his men set sail—much to the relief of their weary hosts. However, the Englishmen ran into a storm and had to return to repair their ships. This time, they were greeted less enthusiastically, for their earlier visit had drained the Hawaiians' supply of food. Trouble developed after some of the islanders took a small boat from one of the ships. In retaliation, Cook tried to take the high chief hostage. A small battle broke out, and Cook was killed.

For the next few years, Hawai'i was left undisturbed by the outside world. But from 1786 on, it was visited more and more frequently by ships from England, France, Russia, Spain, and the United States. A brisk trade between Asia and North America was going on at the time, involving furs from the northwestern United States and silks and teas from China. Hawai'i's location, about halfway between the two continents, made it an ideal stopover for

A 1785 painting depicting the death of Captain Cook

merchant vessels needing to stock up on water and provisions.

Meanwhile, the island chiefs were still fighting among themselves. The battles were bloodier than in earlier years, as the islanders now had guns and cannons procured from the foreign traders.

Unintentionally, the Europeans gave the Hawaiians an even more lethal "gift." Because the islanders had been completely isolated from the Western world, they had no immunities to such illnesses carried by the Europeans as cholera, leprosy, bubonic plague, and even measles and colds. Germs introduced by the sailors swept through the islands, and during the next hundred years, European-brought diseases caused more deaths on the islands than volcanoes, tidal waves, and earthquakes combined. There were at least 250,000 to 300,000 natives on the islands when Cook arrived; by 1872 there were fewer than 60,000.

Chapter 5

THE KINGDOM OF HAWAI'I

THE KINGDOM OF HAWAI'I

KAMEHAMEHA THE GREAT

Kamehameha was a high-ranking warrior from the Big Island who had distinguished himself during the battles on Maui. During his youth, he had learned spear throwing, wrestling, and other skills of warfare. The young man was an important chief in the high chief's court when Captain Cook arrived on the Big Island. Kamehameha was open-minded and eager to learn the ways of these visitors. He was particularly curious about some of the things the *haole* brought with them—especially their cannons and their ships. He quickly realized how helpful these modern arms and vessels would be in interisland skirmishes. He asked the Europeans many questions about military matters. At the same time, he worked to increase his political power among his own people.

Kamehameha rigged his double-hulled canoe to make it look like a Western schooner and armed it with two cannons. With the military knowledge and weaponry he had obtained from the Europeans, he set out to make himself king of all the islands. First he consolidated his power on the island of Hawai'i; then he conquered Maui and O'ahu. By 1795, he had established the Kingdom of Hawai'i, which unified six of the eight major islands.

The Hawaiian people believed that Kamehameha had the gods on his side. One event in particular seemed to prove this. During a battle on the Big Island, the volcano Kīlauea erupted. Many of Kamehameha's enemies were hit and killed by chunks of burning lava. It was obvious to the Hawaiians that the fire goddess, Pele, had come to Kamehameha's assistance. It is interesting that this was the only time on record, among many, many eruptions of Kīlauea, that numerous deaths occurred.

In 1810, Kaumuali'i, the ruler of the islands of Kaua'i and Ni'ihau, agreed to serve under Kamehameha and become part of the Kingdom of Hawai'i. Kamehameha ruled until his death in 1819. He proved to be a great leader. He is remembered as both a fierce young warrior who defeated the other chiefs by force, and as a wise and benevolent king who unified the islands of Hawai'i.

THE END OF *KAPU*

Kamehameha's successor, his eldest son Liholiho, became King Kamehameha II. He ruled for only five years, from 1819 to 1824, but during that time he made an extremely important decision.

Contact with people of different cultures was causing the people of Hawai'i to become disillusioned with their old belief in many vengeful gods and with the strict laws and traditions of *kapu*. Liholiho shared leadership duties with his father's favored wife, Ka'ahumanu. She held the title of *kuhina nui*, which means "important minister." She and other chiefesses pressured Liholiho to overthrow the *kapu* system in order to elevate the status of women. To show his willingness to do so, Liholiho sat down and ate with these high-ranking women at a public feast. Nothing terrible happened, so he issued orders to break other *kapu* laws.

This abrupt renunciation of the old religion was startling, and it left the people unsure about what to believe. Coincidentally, a group of *haole* who lived half an ocean away, in New England,

A nineteenth-century woodcut showing Protestant missionary Hiram Bingham preaching to native Hawaiians at Waimea

had already planned to provide the Hawaiians with a new religion. Protestant missionaries were already on board a ship bound for the Hawaiian Islands.

THE MISSIONARIES AND KAMEHAMEHA II

The fourteen men and women who stepped off the brig *Thaddeus* onto the Kona Coast of the Big Island on April 4, 1820, were not prepared for what they saw. The native islanders were tall and brawny. They wore very little clothing, and the constant sunshine had toned their skins to a deep bronze color. These proper New Englanders, who had left a cold, northern winter behind, probably viewed the Hawaiians as somewhat uncivilized.

Liholiho agreed to let the Protestant missionaries preach Christianity to the islanders. He had no idea that sweeping changes would come to Hawai'i as a result of this one decision.

The missionaries set about their work with great zeal, and succeeded in converting most of the Hawaiians to Christianity. They also set out to change the way the islanders dressed, especially the women. The royal women wore several layers of tapa cloth wrapped around the waist and reaching below the knees, but wore little or nothing above the waist. Surprisingly, they did not object to changing their style of dress. In fact, their

The Protestant missionaries who came to Hawai'i in the 1800s built missions (right), converted thousands of Hawaiians to Christianity, and even changed the way Hawaiian women dressed (left).

previous contact with foreigners had made them eager to be in step with Western fashion.

Through trade with the Orient, the islanders had already acquired beautiful silks and fabrics. Using these fabrics, the missionary women designed floor-length, loose-fitting dresses with long sleeves and taught the Hawaiian women to sew them.

Liholiho and his queen decided to travel to England to meet King George IV. Unfortunately, both the Hawaiian king and his wife caught the measles and died while in London. The king's younger brother, Kauikeaouli (Kamehameha III), became his successor. However, since Kamehameha III was only ten years old at the time, Ka'ahumanu, as queen regent, was the real power behind the throne for a while.

Ka'ahumanu became an enthusiastic convert to Christianity. During the early years of Kamehameha III's reign, many more missionaries came to the islands. They built churches and schools, created a written alphabet for the Hawaiian language, and published Bibles and textbooks. They also set up separate boys' and girls' boarding schools for children of Hawaiian royalty.

Little by little, by teaching and converting the royal families and chiefs, the missionaries gained political power. Given advisory posts in government, they began influencing Hawai'i's laws and altering the structure of Hawaiian society.

Ka'ahumanu's brother, also a convert to Christianity, was governor of the island of O'ahu. He enforced strict, new laws—such as those that forbade adultery or required one to observe the Sabbath—that were quite alien to traditional Hawaiian culture.

Less than a decade after the first missionaries arrived, Protestantism was established as the official religion of Hawai'i. Catholic missionaries arrived at the islands in the late 1820s, but they were forced to leave in 1831. The teaching of the Catholic religion became forbidden, and some Hawaiians who had converted to Catholicism were imprisoned.

Before long, the Protestant missionaries found they needed to raise more money in order to keep their schools and churches open. The American Board of Missions, which had furnished the original financing for the Hawaiian project, was cutting back on the funds sent to the islands. Some missionaries and their descendants began to invest in sugar mills and other local businesses.

KAMEHAMEHA III—A PERIOD OF SWEEPING CHANGES

The Reverend Hiram Bingham, who had led the first group of Protestant missionaries to Hawai'i, remained their unofficial leader until he left the islands in 1840. He and many of his co-workers were concerned about the influence of foreign traders and whalers on the people of Hawai'i. The missionaries felt that the small, weak nation could be easily exploited by other governments and unscrupulous businessmen. The only way to

In this 1852 portrait of the Hawaiian royal family, King Kamehameha III (center) is flanked by two future kings: Alexander Liholiho (top right) and Lot Kamehameha (top left).

prevent this, they reasoned, was to allow Hawai'i's native populace to gain control of their political and economic institutions. Up until this time, however, the common people had no power at all; the Hawaiian royalty owned all the land and ran the government.

The great world powers were closing in on the Pacific territories. In 1839, a French warship blockaded the port of Honolulu and forced the government to grant freedom of worship to Catholics.

The Hawaiian royal government was falling increasingly under the influence of the American missionaries. Soon after the French blockade, Kamehameha III signed a declaration recognizing the rights of all his subjects to "life, limb, the labor of his hands and productions of his mind," and providing equal protection under the law for both chiefs and commoners. The declaration of rights was followed in 1840 by a constitution that was written by a group of highly educated young Hawaiian men. The new document established a supreme court and a bicameral (two-house) legislature. The upper house consisted of members of the royalty; the lower house would be elected by the common people.

Warships from France, England, and the United States were roaming the waters of the Pacific Ocean. The king and his advisors were anxious to persuade these nations to formally recognize Hawai'i's status as an independent nation. The United States did so in 1842. But when England annexed New Zealand, and France seized the South Pacific islands of Tahiti and the Marquesas, it looked as if Hawai'i, too, would fall into foreign hands.

In February 1843, Lord George Paulet arrived on a British frigate and began making demands. Kamehameha III bowed to pressure and signed papers ceding Hawai'i to Great Britain. The Hawaiian flag was lowered and the British Union Jack was hoisted. However, after five months, Hawaiian rule was restored, with guarantees for the rights of British citizens. In November, both England and France officially recognized Hawai'i's independence.

As time went on, Kamehameha III appointed more and more foreigners to important government positions in an attempt to help his country catch up with the Western world. Those who accepted government posts took an oath of allegiance and became naturalized citizens of the kingdom. Dr. Gerrit P. Judd, a medical missionary, resigned from the mission and became one of the king's most trusted advisors. He served in the king's cabinet and helped recruit other foreign-born leaders.

In 1848, under mounting pressure from the sugar planters, Kamehameha III made another sweeping change in the traditional organization of Hawaiian society. Up until this time, all Hawaiian

Hawaiian rural scene, about 1855

land had been considered property of the king. Under a new law, however, the land was divided into three parts. The Great *Māhele*, as this land division was called, kept one portion of the land for the king and his heirs, gave another part to the government, and distributed the rest among the chiefs.

The land division greatly benefited foreigners, who were soon permitted to buy Hawaiian land. They acquired thousands of acres from land-rich but cash-poor royalty who desired money with which to buy imported goods. In 1850, a law was passed that allowed commoners to claim the small pieces of land, or *kuleanas*, that they had lived on or cultivated. But many commoners did not fully understand the new concept of private land ownership. They failed to file land claims or were refused their claims. Some left to find work in port towns and lost their land; others sold their land to foreigners. Today, only a small percentage of *kuleana* lands belongs to native Hawaiians.

King Kamehameha III died in 1854. Here is what his successor said about him:

King Kamehameha IV and his wife, Queen Emma

The age of Kamehamcha III was that of progress and liberty—of schools and of civilization. He gave us a Constitution and fixed laws; he secured the people in the title to their lands, and removed the last chain of oppression. He gave them a voice in his councils and in the making of laws by which they are governed. He was a great national benefactor, and has left the impress of his mild and amiable disposition on the age for which he was born.

KAMEHAMEHA IV

Alexander Liholiho, nephew of Kamehameha III (and grandson of Kamehameha the Great), was the designated heir to the throne. His reign lasted a little less than nine years.

Kamehameha IV was fonder of England than he was of the United States. One reason for this was that he had traveled in both countries and had been treated much more courteously in

England. Racial prejudice, he felt, ran deeper in America than in England. The king was impressed by the Church of England (also called the Anglican or Episcopal church). He donated land and money to found an Anglican church in Hawai'i. He, his queen, Emma, and several members of the cabinet joined that church.

The royal couple had a son, Prince Albert, who died at the age of four. The king's grief over this tragedy contributed to his own death at the early age of twenty-nine.

WHALING SHIPS AND PLANTATIONS

Sandalwood had been the first natural resource to bring foreign money and goods to Hawai'i, and a few years after foreign ships first began stopping at the islands, the sandalwood forests were nearly wiped out.

The next source of revenue—whaling—was discovered in the 1820s. Today the world is heavily dependent on petroleum oil; whale oil had the same importance in the early 1800s. Whalebone and blubber were also in demand. The waters of the Pacific seemed to hold an endless supply of these valuable mammals, and hundreds of whaling ships from faraway countries sailed into the ports of Honolulu and Lahaina in search of fresh water, supplies, and entertainment.

Despite the best efforts of the missionaries to wipe out what they considered sinful behavior, Hawai'i became a favorite spot for sailors from the whaling ships to carouse and drink. One traveler called Lahaina, on Maui, "one of the breathing holes of hell . . . a sight to make a missionary weep."

For about thirty-five years, the money brought into Hawai'i by the whalers was the major source of outside income. Then, in the 1860s, three factors caused the whaling industry to go into a rapid

In the 1820s, the whaling industry became Hawai'i's major source of revenue.

decline. Whales were becoming scarce because they had been overhunted. Other, cheaper products, such as petroleum and coal, began taking the place of whale oil as the most popular form of fuel for heating and lighting. And as the Civil War began, New England whaling ships were converted into merchant fleets or left in harbor until the fighting was over.

After the war was over, the production of sugar gradually replaced whaling as the mainstay of the Hawaiian economy. The population of the West Coast of the United States was growing rapidly, providing Hawai'i with a strong market for sugar and other agricultural products. By the late 1800s, most of Hawai'i's sugarcane crop was being shipped to the United States.

The development of agriculture on large plantations had an impact on Hawaiian society that extended far beyond the economic one. Many workers were needed to plant and harvest

Field workers at Līhu'e, Kaua'i, in 1890

the sugarcane, transport it to the mills, and refine it for sale. The plantation owners soon found that there were not enough Hawaiian workers to fill these jobs. Consequently, in the 1850s, Chinese laborers were imported by the thousands. As the industry grew, more and more laborers were needed. Polynesians from the South Pacific were brought to Hawai'i in 1859. Japanese workers first arrived in the late 1860s. These immigrants came to the islands under a contract system that required them to work on the Hawaiian plantations for at least three years or face imprisonment. In the 1870s, these plantation workers were joined by German and Portuguese immigrants.

KAMEHAMEHA V

Lot Kamehameha, the younger brother of Alexander Liholiho, succeeded to the throne as Kamehameha V in 1863. Kamehameha V was more interested in preserving traditional Hawaiian values

For sixteen years, Father Damien (right) cared for the leprosy patients on Moloka'i, helping them build homes, a small hospital, and a church (left).

and customs than his brother had been. He called a convention for the purpose of drawing up a new constitution that would return more power to the throne.

During Lot's reign, the government borrowed a great deal of money, at very high interest rates, in order to build a number of important public structures. The national debt became very large for such a small kingdom.

FATHER DAMIEN, THE MARTYR MISSIONARY

Among the many diseases brought to Hawai'i by early foreign visitors was leprosy, now called Hansen's disease. Hawaiians called the malady *ma'i Pake*, "the Chinese disease," though there is no evidence that it was brought to the islands from China. Leprosy was known and dreaded in many parts of the world from ancient times until the 1940s, when certain drugs were found to treat it. In its advanced stages, the disease can cause deformity, paralysis, and blindness.

Leprosy was introduced to the islands sometime around 1830. Thirty years later, the government began isolating all diseased persons on the north coast of Moloka'i. In 1873, a young priest from Belgium, Father Joseph Damien de Veuster, came to the desolate leper colony. He helped the victims to help themselves by clearing the land and growing crops. They built homes, a church, and a small hospital.

Father Damien served the people of the colony for sixteen years, until he himself died of the disease. After his death, he became known throughout the world as the "Martyr of Moloka'i."

A NEW KING IS ELECTED

Lot Kamehameha never married. When he died in 1872, the line of direct descendants of Kamehameha the Great ended, and there was no clear successor to the throne. One of the major candidates under consideration was Prince William Lunalilo, a cousin of the late king. Popular and well educated, he decided to try to assume the throne by legal means, through a popular election. He won the election by a large margin, and the legislature then confirmed him as well.

Lunalilo had very little experience or knowledge of political and financial matters. He was more sympathetic to the Americans living in Hawai'i than his immediate predecessors had been, and he named several able Americans to his cabinet.

Lunalilo's reign was a very short one; he died a little over a year after taking office. Like Lot Kamehameha, he had been a bachelor and left no heir to the throne.

A EUROPEAN-STYLE MONARCH

David Kalākaua, an educated and polished gentleman who was a descendant of Hawaiian chiefs, was elected to be the new

King Kalākaua, an elected monarch, reigned from 1874 to 1891.

monarch. He was thirty-eight years old at the time, and he served as king for seventeen years.

Kalākaua enjoyed the pomp and ceremony of royalty, and he was more impressed with European nobility than with American democracy and Protestantism. The Americans in Honolulu were somewhat uneasy about his election. However, they were even more distrustful of his major opponent, Queen Emma (the widow of Kamehameha IV), who was very open about her love for the British.

Kalākaua's election set off a short-lived riot staged by Queen Emma's supporters. The new king asked for help from American armed forces to put down the rebellion, and 150 American troops, along with 70 Englishmen, soon dispersed the crowd.

The history of Kalākaua's reign is controversial. Some historians have considered him an intelligent leader who helped perpetuate Hawaiian cultural traditions and added much to his country's prestige; others see him as a luxury-loving and self-centered spendthrift.

Kalākaua quickly formed a cabinet of foreigners from several nations—America, England, and Germany. In 1874, as a further diplomatic gesture, he made a trip to Washington, D.C. There he was received by President Ulysses S. Grant and a joint session of Congress. Kalākaua was the first reigning monarch of any nation to visit the United States, and he was lavishly entertained.

The Hawaiian government and the sugar planters had been trying to bring about a trade agreement between the United States and Hawai'i for a long time. Kalākaua's visit helped this cause. In 1875, the two countries signed an important reciprocity treaty. The United States agreed to remove a tariff (tax) on incoming shipments of Hawaiian sugar. This made the sugar cheaper for American buyers, thus assuring Hawaiian sugar growers of a secure market for their product. In return, Kalākaua agreed to allow only the United States to use Hawai'i's ports and harbors.

In 1881, Kalākaua made a widely publicized trip around the world. He was warmly received and extravagantly entertained everywhere—in Japan, China, Siam, Singapore, Malaysia, Burma, India, Egypt, a half-dozen European countries, and the United States.

Before leaving on his tour, Kalākaua had decided that the monarchy deserved a new royal palace. The cornerstone was laid for 'Iolani Palace, a dignified and handsome building, and the structure was completed in late 1882. The king then decided that he wanted a grand coronation ceremony, similar to those given to European rulers, for himself and his queen. These and other expenditures put the king deeply into debt.

On the ninth anniversary of his election to the throne, King Kalākaua held a European-style coronation for himself outside 'Iolani Palace.

The Americans living in Hawai'i were becoming more and more disillusioned with Kalākaua. In 1887, they took part in an armed rebellion and forced the king to accept a new constitution that turned over much of the political power to the *haole*. Only men who owned at least $3,000 worth of property or had an income of $600 or more a year were to be allowed to vote. This excluded most of the kingdom's nonwhite residents.

During the same year, the United States was granted exclusive rights to use Pearl Harbor as a naval base. These events paved the way for further American influence over the islands. By the time Kalākaua died in 1891, the powers of the monarchy had been reduced considerably.

Queen Lili'uokalani (left) was Hawai'i's first reigning queen and last monarch. She ruled from 1891 until 1893, when the monarchy was overthrown by a group of Honolulu businessmen.
This cartoon (above) comments on the annexation of Hawai'i by the United States in 1898.

THE END OF THE KINGDOM

Kalākaua had named his sister, Princess Lydia Lili'uokalani, heir to the throne. Upon his death, she became Hawai'i's first reigning queen—and the last ruler of the kingdom.

Queen Lili'uokalani realized that what the American businessmen really wanted was to make her kingdom a territory of the United States, and she was determined not to let this happen. She wanted to restore the constitution of 1864 and regain control of the government for the monarchy and the Hawaiian people. By this time, however, diseases had taken such a toll on the native Hawaiians that there were fewer of them in Hawai'i than there were foreigners and people of mixed heritage. Also, much of the property and nearly all the financial power was in the hands of foreigners.

In January of 1893, a small group of Americans and Europeans, aided by United States Marines, took over the Hawaiian government without any bloodshed. Sanford B. Dole, a Honolulu-born American lawyer, was declared governor of the Provisional Government of Hawaii. The queen was unable to stop the overthrow of her kingdom.

The American sugar planters wanted the United States to annex Hawai'i because it would ensure a firm market for their product. However, United States President Grover Cleveland, shocked at the news of the revolution, refused the provisional government's request for annexation. After five and a half months, the provisional government proclaimed that the islands were now to be considered the Republic of Hawai'i, with Dole as its president. Queen Lili'uokalani was held under house arrest in 'Iolani Palace for five years.

When President Cleveland lost the 1896 presidential election to Republican candidate William McKinley, Hawai'i's fate was sealed. In 1898, McKinley signed a resolution that made Hawai'i a possession of the United States. Cleveland later wrote, "Hawai'i is ours. As I look back upon the first steps in this miserable business and as I contemplate the means used to complete the outrage, I am ashamed of the whole affair."

However, Hawai'i might have lost its independence even if the Americans had not interfered. The government was nearly bankrupt. Diseases had severely reduced the size of the native population. Several major world powers were lurking about, ready to protect their interests by force, if necessary. In a single century, Western civilization had poured over the islands like a tidal wave that could not be held back.

Chapter 6
THE LONG ROAD TO STATEHOOD

THE LONG ROAD TO STATEHOOD

THE TERRITORY OF HAWAI'I

An act of Congress in 1900 made it official. Hawai'i was a United States territory. A territorial legislature would enact local laws, but Congress had the power to change or veto any of them. Although all islanders were now American citizens, the territory had no representation in Congress. The president of the United States would appoint the governor and other top government officials.

Three other United States territories existed at that time: Alaska, Arizona, and New Mexico. A pattern of westward expansion in the United States had begun in 1787 with the passage of the Northwest Ordinance. Newly acquired areas were first declared territories; then, when enough people had settled an area, a petition for statehood could be sent to Congress. New states would be on an equal footing with the original thirteen.

Sanford Dole was appointed the first governor of the territory. Dole was confident, as were most other islanders, that statehood would follow soon for all four existing territories. No one could have dreamed that it would take nearly six decades for Alaska and Hawai'i to achieve statehood.

Annexation by the United States gave the islanders American citizenship—with an important exception. Through several laws known as the Oriental Exclusion Acts, passed in the late 1800s,

Congress had barred all foreign-born Asians from becoming United States citizens. More than half of Hawai'i's residents at the time of annexation were either Japanese or Chinese. Nearly 25 percent were Hawaiian or part Hawaiian; 17 percent were Caucasian. These last two groups became the only ones permitted to have any political power over local affairs.

The territorial legislature began petitioning Congress for statehood in 1903 and continued to do so, over and over again, through the years. Although several congressional committees recommended granting statehood, some members of Congress strongly opposed it. Most of the opposition was based on racial prejudice and fear that the islands' residents of Asian ancestry might not support the United States in the event of war.

A few families, most of whom were involved in the sugar industry, made huge fortunes during the early years of the territory. They became the new ruling class of Hawai'i, leading the islands' political, social, and business affairs.

In the early 1900s, pineapples became a second major crop in Hawai'i. During this time, a new wave of immigrants that included Puerto Ricans, Koreans, and Filipinos arrived to work on the plantations. By this time, a clear, unofficial caste system had developed in Hawai'i's multiethnic society. The best jobs and highest social and political positions were held by the *haole*— people of American, English, Scottish, and German ancestry. The Hawaiians had the next-highest social status, followed by the Portuguese (who were not accepted as true *haole*), the Chinese, the Japanese, and the Filipinos.

Many of the contract workers who had arrived in the late 1800s had returned home after working out the terms of their employment. Others, especially Chinese and Japanese, stayed in Hawai'i. Many continued to work as farm laborers long enough to

Between 1852 and 1905, some 184,000 immigrants came to Hawai'i to work on the plantations. By the early 1900s, Hawai'i's labor force was made up of people from a wide variety of ethnic backgrounds, including Japanese (top left), Spanish and Portuguese (top right), and Filipinos (left).

save enough money to leave the plantations for the towns and cities, where they started their own small businesses. These new islanders worked hard to achieve a better life for their children. They sent them to school and encouraged them to pursue professional careers.

MILITARY BASES

One of the main reasons the United States had been interested in controlling Hawai'i was to have a strategic military outpost in the Pacific. The army lost no time in establishing bases on the islands. Fort Shafter, near Pearl Harbor, became the first permanent garrison. Other forts quickly followed on O'ahu — Armstrong, De Russy, Ruger, Kamehameha, and Weaver.

Pearl Harbor, large and nearly landlocked, is one of the finest harbors in the world. In 1908, the navy dredged a narrow channel from the ocean into the harbor and built a base beside it.

World War I brought several military aviation centers to the islands. Ford Island Air Station, in the middle of Pearl Harbor, was used as a base for seaplanes.

Before the United States entered the conflict, several German merchant ships and military vessels sought shelter in Honolulu Harbor. Eventually, the United States government told the German officers that they must leave the harbor or be held there for the duration of the war. They chose to remain, and the crews were placed in detention.

In 1917, the United States declared war on Germany. Almost ten thousand islanders joined the armed services.

Civilian groups in Hawai'i took part in such patriotic efforts as raising funds and recruiting volunteer workers for the Red Cross, buying war bonds, and stepping up food production. The old

On October 22, 1936, the *Hawaii Clipper*, the first plane to carry paying passengers from the United States mainland to Hawai'i, landed in Honolulu.

Royal Hawaiian Hotel, transformed into an army and navy YMCA, was used as headquarters for many committees and groups.

BETWEEN THE TWO WORLD WARS

Modern means of communication and transportation expanded rapidly all over the world during the 1920s and 1930s. Hawai'i's ties with the outside world grew stronger as its first commercial radio stations began broadcasting, airplanes started flying across the ocean from the mainland and between the islands, and telephone service with the mainland was put into operation. In 1935, commercial air service across the Pacific between North America and Asia was initiated. Hawai'i, the "Crossroads of the Pacific," was a convenient stopover for international air traffic—just as it had long been for ocean liners and cargo ships.

The Great Depression of the 1930s had a severe effect on Hawai'i. Many people were out of work. The pineapple industry, which had been second to sugar in economic importance in Hawai'i, was especially hard hit. People simply could not afford to buy the luxurious tropical fruit, and many agricultural workers lost their jobs.

The USS *Arizona* burns furiously during the Japanese attack on Pearl Harbor.

Powerful sugar companies on the mainland persuaded Congress to pass a law limiting Hawai'i's production of sugar. Islanders were furious; this quota system treated them as if they were foreigners, not citizens. In spite of this law, the sugar industry held up better than some of Hawai'i's other businesses.

"JAPAN HAS BOMBED PEARL HARBOR"

Many Americans on the mainland barely knew where Hawai'i was before December 7, 1941. Then suddenly, within twenty-four hours, every radio and newspaper headline in the nation shouted the shocking news that the air force of the Empire of Japan had attacked the United States naval base at Pearl Harbor.

Even though a world war had been raging in Europe for more than two years, the United States was not yet directly involved. To most Americans, military and civilian alike, this air attack came as a complete surprise. It began at about 7:55 on that fateful Sunday morning, and for the next two hours, Japanese bombs rained down on Pearl Harbor. When it was over, some 2,335 servicemen and 68 civilians had been killed, 188 airplanes had been destroyed, and 18 naval vessels had been sunk or crippled. Never before in the nation's history had so much loss of life and military strength occurred within such a short period of time.

By late afternoon, Hawai'i had been placed under martial law. In less than a day, life on the once-tranquil tropical islands was transformed. On Monday, December 8, President Franklin Roosevelt and the United States Congress officially declared war on Japan.

Military rule was maintained on the islands for more than three and a half years, until the war was nearly over. Newspapers and mail were censored and food and gasoline were rationed. Curfews and blackout regulations were enforced. At night, no lights could be used outside or be left burning behind uncovered windows. Complete darkness was necessary to make it difficult for enemy planes to find a target. All terms of employment and wages were frozen as of December 7. The army registered and fingerprinted every island resident over the age of six, and everyone was required to carry an identification card.

"GO FOR BROKE"

Living under martial law made the war years difficult for all islanders. For almost three years, Hawai'i's government, police force, and court system were controlled by the United States Army, and many normal civil liberties were trampled on. Hawai'i became the headquarters of the Pacific war effort, and servicemen stationed in Hawai'i doubled the territory's population in just four years. Housing became scarce and seriously overcrowded.

The Japanese community in Hawai'i had unique problems. More than one-third of the people living on the islands at the outbreak of war were of Japanese ancestry. Even though many were American citizens who had never even visited Japan, wartime tensions and bitterness toward the country that had bombed Pearl Harbor created widespread resentment toward all those of Japanese descent.

The surprise attack raised fears that Japan might actually invade Hawai'i, or even the West Coast of the American mainland. Several high-ranking military officers suspected that the Japanese air force had been assisted by Japanese Americans living in Hawai'i. Anti-Japanese bigotry in the western states of California, Oregon, and Washington gathered such strength that some 112,000 Japanese Americans were forced to leave their homes and move to one of ten hastily constructed relocation centers. About 1,400 Japanese Americans from Hawai'i were sent to the centers.

Government actions and attitudes toward the Japanese Americans—in both Hawai'i and on the West Coast—were based entirely on wartime hysteria, not on fact. Not a single act of espionage or sabotage by a Japanese American was ever discovered. The evacuation of 112,000 innocent people from the western states was said to be a "necessity." Yet in Hawai'i—2,000 miles (3,219 kilometers) closer to Japan—the government decided that it was a "necessity" *not* to evacuate the majority of Japanese Americans. At the time, Japanese made up 40 percent of Hawai'i's population and work force; their contribution to the economy was too great for the government to justify removing them from the islands.

Determined to prove their loyalty to the United States, Japanese

Twenty-six hundred Japanese American volunteers from Hawai'i attend a farewell ceremony at 'Iolani Palace in 1943.

Americans in Hawai'i volunteered for the army in droves. About 1,500 Japanese Americans were already serving in the United States Army at the time of the attack on Pearl Harbor. About six months later, many of these soldiers became part of the newly organized 100th Infantry Battalion. They were sent to the mainland for training. Later, more than 2,800 other Japanese Americans, most of whom were from Hawai'i, joined the army to form the 442nd Regimental Combat Team.

The 100th was sent to battle in Africa and Italy, where its heroic performances earned it the nickname the "Purple Heart Battalion." The 442nd was united with the 100th in Italy, and the unit took part in seven major campaigns in Europe. The 100/442 Regimental Combat Team became the most decorated American military unit of World War II. The battalion's motto was "Go For Broke," an expression used by Hawaiian dice-shooters when they wanted to gamble all their money on one roll of the dice. To the men of the 100/442, it meant "Give it your all" or "Don't stop fighting until you've done everything you possibly can."

STATEHOOD AT LAST

After World War II, Hawai'i's political leaders renewed their efforts to go forward from territorial status to statehood. Congressional bills calling for the admission of both Alaska and Hawai'i as new states were introduced several times without success. Then, another conflict interfered. From 1950 to 1953, Hawai'i became an important base for American forces involved in the Korean conflict.

Finally, in 1959, Congress agreed to allow Hawai'i to become the fiftieth state of the United States of America. President Eisenhower officially admitted Hawai'i into the Union on August 21, 1959. The racial diversity of Hawai'i was reflected in the first state elections. William F. Quinn, a *haole*, was sworn in as the state's first governor. James K. Kealoha, of Hawaiian descent, became the lieutenant governor. One of the first two United States senators from Hawai'i was Hiram L. Fong, a Chinese American. Daniel K. Inouye, a Japanese American, became the state's first congressman.

TOURISM—A NEW SOURCE OF WEALTH

World War II had been for Hawai'i what historians call a "watershed." Many things changed forever. New ways of earning a living came to be commonplace. The sugar and pineapple plantations gradually lost their place as Hawai'i's principal employers.

Tourism is one of several industries that have brought about great changes on the islands. Many new residents have come to the islands along with the visitors; the population has more than doubled since 1940. Construction and such services as

On March 12, 1959, people all over Hawai'i celebrated the news that Congress had finally approved Hawai'i's admission as a state.

transportation and communication have grown to keep pace with the growing population.

Hawai'i's businessmen had begun promoting the islands as a tourist destination in the 1890s. They knew that the beauty of the landscape, the near-perfect climate, and the relaxing island lifestyle would appeal to almost any visitor.

Nearly ten thousand visitors came to the tropical islands in 1922. These numbers increased each year, and the future for Hawai'i's tourist industry looked bright until the depression of the 1930s slowed things down. Gradually, as the economy improved, business picked up again. In 1941, just before the

Tourism in the Aloha State boomed after World II.

United States entered World War II, Hawai'i attracted an all-time high of thirty-two thousand visitors. Honolulu had only five hotels at the time, and only two of those were on now-popular Waikīkī Beach.

Hawai'i's tourism industry received an important boost at the end of the war, when the military presented the territory with several fully functioning airports. Within several months, Pan American World Airways, British Commonwealth Airlines, and Philippine Airlines began regular commercial service to Hawai'i. Several other airlines followed within the next few years. Because airfares were lower than ocean-liner fares had been, many middle-income people were now able to afford a vacation in Hawai'i. The thousands of servicemen who had passed through or were stationed in Hawai'i during World War II and the Korean conflict were well acquainted with its beauty, and many were anxious to come back during peacetime.

One of Hawai'i's greatest boosters was popular radio and television personality Arthur Godfrey. Godfrey had come to the islands as a war correspondent in the 1940s, and in his broadcasts, he talked frequently about their beauty and the friendliness of their people. He strummed many a tropical tune on his *'ukulele*, and his enthusiasm for everything about the islands made *aloha* shirts, flower *leis*, and Hawaiian music popular on the mainland.

As planeload after planeload of visitors landed in Honolulu, the need for new facilities became obvious. Construction of new hotels became a major activity. At first most of the hotels and resorts were built on O'ahu, but eventually the other islands started to benefit from Hawai'i's newfound popularity as well.

Most people like to shop while on vacation. Hawai'i businessman Walter Dillingham decided to provide visitors to Hawai'i, as well as islanders, with a modern and convenient place to spend their money. The Ala Moana Shopping Center in Honolulu opened in 1959. At the time, it was the largest shopping center in the world.

By the 1980s, only federal government expenditures—much of them for the military—were more important to the economy of the islands than tourism. Hotels, restaurants, nightclubs, stores, airlines, bus-tour companies, car-rental agencies, bike-rental shops, charter boats, sightseeing helicopters, and a variety of tourist attractions are among the dozens of businesses that benefit from tourism.

Most of Hawai'i's visitors come from the mainland United States and Canada, but increasing numbers are coming from the Far East and the South Pacific.

On almost any given day, more than a hundred thousand visitors are enjoying the balmy Hawaiian weather, lying on the beaches, wandering through the shops, and looking at the sights. And one visit isn't enough for most of them; nearly half have been to Hawai'i at least once before.

Chapter 7

GOVERNMENT AND THE ECONOMY

GOVERNMENT AND THE ECONOMY

GOVERNMENT

Hawai'i's state government is structured much like those of the other forty-nine states. However, Hawai'i's small size has allowed it to operate under a more streamlined system of government than is found in many of the other states.

Only two state officials, the governor and the lieutenant governor, are elected to the executive branch. The directors of most of the seventeen executive departments are appointed by the governor with the approval of the senate.

Hawai'i's legislature consists of a fifty-one-member house of representatives and a twenty-five-member senate. Legislators are elected from legislative districts that are divided so that each one has roughly the same number of residents. Representatives are elected to serve two-year terms. Senators serve for four years, and one-half of the senate seats come up for election every two years.

Hawai'i's judicial system includes a supreme court, an appellate court, four circuit courts, and twenty-seven district courts. The five justices of the supreme court and the judges of the appellate and circuit courts are appointed for ten-year terms by the governor. District magistrates are appointed to six-year terms by the chief justice of the supreme court.

There is only one level of local government in Hawai'i—the

county. Hawai'i has no self-governing, incorporated cities or towns. County governments provide the services that in other states are administered by such smaller bodies as townships, cities, or villages.

There are four principal counties: Hawai'i (the Big Island), Maui (which includes the islands of Maui, Lāna'i, Kaho'olawe and most of Moloka'i), Kaua'i (Kaua'i and Ni'ihau), and the City and County of Honolulu (O'ahu and the northwestern Hawaiian islands). Each county has an elected council and a mayor.

A fifth county, Kalawao, is entirely under the jurisdiction of the Department of Health. It includes the section of Moloka'i that was set aside long ago for victims of Hansen's disease.

EDUCATION

Hawai'i is the only state with a single, statewide board of education. This elected board appoints a superintendent to administer the state public-school system, which includes 7 school districts, some 230 public elementary and secondary schools; and several adult-education facilities. Lahainaluna High School on West Maui, built by mission students in 1831, is the oldest American high school west of the Rocky Mountains.

Hawai'i has a large number of private elementary and secondary schools, many of which have a religious affiliation. Some date back to the early missionary days.

The Kamehameha Schools are a world-famous complex of elementary and secondary schools in Honolulu. They were established through a huge estate left by Princess Bernice Pauahi Bishop, a Hawaiian chiefess; and her husband Charles Reed Bishop, an American banker. Princess Pauahi's intent was to make first-class education available to children of Hawaiian descent.

A Japanese tea ceremony at the East-West Center, an institute established to promote understanding among the people of Asia, the Pacific, and the United States

Because Hawaiian residents represent so many different ethnic backgrounds, cross-cultural and multilingual education is encouraged. Japanese, Chinese, and Korean language schools are among the educational opportunities available. Hawai'i also has a number of trade schools and special schools for severely disabled individuals.

The University of Hawaii operates six community colleges and three university campuses. Its main campus in Honolulu enrolls some twenty thousand students. The university is especially noted for its programs in tropical agriculture, astronomy, and ocean-related and Pacific-Asian studies. The Center for Cultural and Technical Interchange Between East and West, known as the East-West Center, is a unique international college and training center.

In Lā'ie, O'ahu, the Mormon church operates a Hawai'i branch of Brigham Young University. The state also has another private university, Chaminade University of Honolulu; and two private colleges.

Tourists (shown here learning the *hula*) are an important asset to Hawai'i's economy.

SERVICE INDUSTRIES

Today in Hawai'i, service industries employ far more people and provide much greater income for the state than the plantations ever did. Tourism, which brings in more than $4 billion a year, is the state's leading industry.

Defense is the second most important service industry. More than sixty-five thousand military and civilian personnel working for the Department of Defense are based in Hawai'i. The United States Navy, Army, and Air Force all maintain large bases on the islands.

Tourism, government, and other service industries (wholesale and retail trade, finance, insurance, real estate, and community, social, and personal services) account for nearly 90 percent of the state's gross income. Eight out of ten people in Hawai'i's labor force work in service industries.

MANUFACTURING AND CONSTRUCTION

Manufacturing and construction each account for about 5 percent of Hawai'i's gross state income. Food processing, principally sugar, is still the most important; the garment industry ranks second.

Since World War II, several other manufacturing industries have been established in Hawai'i. Many difficulties hamper the growth of manufacturing on the islands. Local supplies of raw materials, as well as local markets, are limited. The cost of transporting both raw materials and finished products makes manufacturing expensive in Hawai'i. Technological progress may ease these problems.

The most promising future for manufacturing in Hawai'i is in producing items that are small in bulk but high in value. Currently, Hawai'i's manufactured items include pineapple fruit, juice, and frozen concentrate; printed materials; clothing; stone, clay, and glass products; chemicals; and fabricated metal products.

AGRICULTURE

Agriculture's economic importance has shrunk drastically in Hawai'i in recent years. Only about 1 percent of the gross state income comes from agriculture.

Sugarcane is still the leading crop, and pineapples still rank second. An agricultural experiment that began in the 1920s has resulted in the harvesting of a product that today is associated with Hawai'i almost as much as sugar and pineapples have been: macadamia nuts. Large-scale planting of macadamia seedlings was done in the late 1940s. These trees must be cared for very carefully, and it takes fifteen years for them to reach full

Hawai'i's agricultural products include cattle (top left), pineapples (bottom left), and ornamental flowers (right).

production. Once mature, however, they produce well. Two companies produce most of the macadamia nuts in Hawai'i, under the brand names Mauna Loa and Hawaiian Holiday.

Other agricultural activities in Hawai'i include the raising of cattle, poultry, horses, hogs, ornamental flowers, and such tropical fruits as bananas, guavas, and papayas. The Kona Coast of the Big Island is famous for its high-quality coffee. Hawai'i is the only state in the nation where coffee is grown.

TRANSPORTATION AND COMMUNICATION

Since Hawai'i is made up of separate islands, its transportation system differs from that of the other forty-nine states. All travel between the islands, as well as the transport of all exports and imports, must be done by air or sea. Many necessities of modern life have to be carried long distances, and the added freight charges make the cost of living in Hawai'i very high.

More than twenty-five major airlines offer trans-Pacific flights to and from Hawai'i. Air travel among the islands is furnished by three airlines. Honolulu International Airport is the state's largest and busiest airport. The Big Island, Maui, and Kaua'i also have airports served by areas outside Hawai'i.

Including the naval shipyard at Pearl Harbor, Hawai'i has seven deep-water ports. The others are Hilo and Kawaihae on Hawai'i, Kahului on Maui, Nāwiliwili and Port Allen on Kaua'i, and Honolulu on O'ahu.

Honolulu has an excellent public bus system. There are no passenger trains in Hawai'i, with the exception of a train on Maui that provides short recreational excursions. The state has about 4,300 miles (6,920 kilometers) of paved roadways.

Hawai'i has about twenty-seven AM radio stations and twenty FM stations. Fourteen commercial and two public television stations operate in the state. Cable viewers are served by about ten companies.

Nine daily newspapers, as well as a number of weekly papers, semiweekly papers, and magazines, serve the state. The two major English-language newspapers are the *Honolulu Advertiser* and the *Honolulu Star-Bulletin*.

The University of Hawai'i Press and several small local publishers produce books.

Chapter 8

ARTS AND RECREATION

ARTS AND RECREATION

The American missionaries established the first formal schools in Hawai'i. At these schools, Hawaiian children were taught American ideas and values. The missionaries tried to substitute their concept of a civilized society for Hawaiian customs that they viewed as barbaric and savage. For example, they discouraged *hula* dancing, which they considered improper. Their efforts to wipe it out never quite succeeded, however.

Even though a process of Americanization has been going on for more than 150 years in Hawai'i, Hawaiian cultural traditions have managed to survive. Other ethnic groups in Hawai'i, especially the Japanese, have also managed to keep their heritages alive.

Today, Hawai'i's educators recognize the richness that comes from having a multiethnic society. Increasingly, the people of Hawai'i are attempting to preserve the various arts, customs, languages, and religions that have been brought to the islands by different groups. This trend has included a renewed interest and pride in native Hawaiian culture.

NATIVE HAWAIIAN ARTS

Ancient Hawaiians drew their artistic inspiration from nature. Their customs were based on the idea of living in harmony with

This wooden bowl (left) and this feather helmet (right) are among the thousands of beautifully crafted Hawaiian objects on display at the Bishop Museum in Honolulu.

nature, not in conquering it. Sacred temple sites were chosen with careful consideration of the surrounding natural landscape.

When these early islanders used natural objects to make things of beauty, they altered the original appearance as little as possible. They polished their shells, gourds, and wooden objects only enough to bring out the patterns and shapes already within them.

Artisans used brightly colored birds' feathers to make a variety of exquisite symbols of royalty. Techniques were developed to snare birds without killing or maiming them. The craftsmen carefully plucked the most beautifully colored feathers, then let the birds fly away.

Although all the Polynesian groups did featherwork, the Hawaiian creations are regarded as the finest of all. Several different items were made of feathers. The floor-length cloaks created for the highest-ranking royalty were the most spectacular products.

Other ancient Hawaiian artwork included wooden sculptures,

The *lei* is one of the best-known symbols of Hawai'i.

tapa cloth covered with intricate designs, and head wreaths and *leis* fashioned of flowers, leaves, vines, seeds, or berries.

Leis are seen everywhere in Hawai'i today. Recognized as a symbol of the islands, they are traditionally presented to friends when they arrive on or leave the islands. They are also used for any special event. On ceremonious occasions, important guests may be presented with *maile leis*. These are long, open-ended strands of braided leaves of the *maile* plant, which has a distinctive spicy aroma.

Many *leis* are simple strings of small orchids or carnations. Others are truly works of art and extremely valuable. They can be made of as many as a thousand tiny blossoms. The rarest and most expensive *leis* are fashioned of feathers or tiny shells.

Classes in *lei*-making are not hard to find. Many islanders make *leis* as a hobby, using flowers from their own gardens.

Each of the eight main islands has its own special type of *lei*: shells for Ni'ihau, *mokihana* (a small, fragrant fruit) for Kaua'i, *'ilima* flowers for O'ahu, *kauna'oa* (a vine with orange stems) for Lāna'i, *hinahina* (a threadlike moss) for Kaho'olawe, flowers of the *kukui* (the state tree) for Moloka'i, *lokelani* (a small red rose) for

A modern-day *hula* class on Kaua'i (left) and the earliest-known photograph of *hula* dancers, from about 1858 (right)

Maui, and *lehua* flowers for the Big Island. Pageants and parades often feature people wearing the *lei* of the island they represent.

THE *HULA*

Like the *lei*, the *hula* is a universally recognized trademark of Hawai'i. In ancient times, it was used as part of a religious service. Both men and women learned to dance, but only men performed in the temples.

In a *hula*, the hand gestures illustrate the words of the chant or song that accompanies it. According to tradition, people would act out events that they hoped would occur in the future. Thus, in a sense, the *hula* was a kind of prayer.

The *hula* was outlawed by the early missionaries, but in the late 1800s, it was revived by King Kalākaua. In 1915, a group of *hula* dancers performed at an international exposition in San Francisco. Almost overnight, the dance became popular throughout North

The *'ukulele* (played by seated man on right), an instrument used in many Hawaiian musical groups, was brought to Hawai'i from Portugal.

America and Europe, and writers of popular music began to imitate Hawaiian melodies.

The *hula* has enjoyed several periods of renewed popularity since then. Hollywood movies of the 1930s featured the *hula*. After World War II, the new resort hotels on the islands began to use a popularized version of the dance in their shows for tourists. This type of *hula* is still performed regularly in Hawai'i's nightclubs and outdoor pageants. The traditional, classical form of the *hula* continues to be studied and performed by serious scholars of the performing arts and native Hawaiian culture.

MUSIC AND THEATER

Along with *leis* and *hula* dancing, one musical instrument is universally associated with Hawai'i: the *'ukulele*. Actually, only the word is Hawaiian. The instrument was brought to the islands by Portuguese immigrants. An Englishman named Edward Purvis, who immigrated to Hawai'i in 1879, became renowned for his outstanding ability to play this small, four-stringed relative of the guitar. His fingers flew across the strings so rapidly that Hawaiian listeners gave him the nickname " *'Ukulele*," which means "leaping flea." The instrument he played soon became known as an *'ukulele*.

The guitar had been introduced to Hawai'i many years before by early whalers. Hawaiian musicians loosened the strings of the instrument and developed a new and distinctive type of guitar music characterized by a sliding, crooning sound. Anyone who has heard both Hawaiian and Spanish guitar music can confirm that the difference between them is unmistakable.

Several Hawaiian monarchs were very influential in promoting Hawaiian music. King Kamehameha V engaged a German musician named Heinrich Berger to form the Royal Hawaiian Band. As director of the group from 1872 to 1915, Berger conducted thousands of concerts. He also arranged more than a thousand Hawaiian songs and wrote seventy-five original pieces of music that followed Hawaiian musical tradition. The Royal Hawaiian Band still exists and performs regularly in a gazebo on the grounds of 'Iolani Palace.

King Kalākaua, who came to the throne in 1874, was a patron of the arts. He had his own musical group and he collaborated with other composers in writing music. He wrote the lyrics to the national anthem of Hawai'i (and now the state song), "Hawai'i Pono'i." His sister, who became Queen Lili'uokalani, wrote one of the best-known Hawaiian songs, "Aloha 'Oe."

Present-day performing arts groups in Hawai'i include the Hawaii Opera Theater, Honolulu Symphony Orchestra, Chamber Music Hawaii, Honolulu Community Theater, University of Hawaii Theatre, Honolulu Theater for Youth, Windward Theater Guild, and Polynesian Cultural Center.

LITERATURE

Several world-famous authors who have spent time in Hawai'i have used the islands as a setting for some of their stories and essays. The work of these writers has helped to make the islands popular.

Mark Twain, author of *The Adventures of Tom Sawyer* and dozens of other books and stories, visited Hawai'i in 1866. While there, he wrote a series of travel letters that were published in the *Sacramento Union*. Some of these letters, as well as other material about Hawai'i, later appeared in his book *Roughing It*. Twain traveled in O'ahu, Maui, and the Big Island. He especially loved Maui and wrote glowingly about the experience of watching the sun rise over Haleakalā Crater.

Robert Louis Stevenson, whose writings included popular books about the South Seas, came to Hawai'i in 1889 and stayed at the Sans Souci resort hotel on Waikīkī Beach. He wrote in the hotel's guest book, praising the scenery, the pure air, the food, and the "heavenly sunsets hung out . . . over the Pacific and the distant hills of Wai'anae."

Stevenson became involved in a local controversy soon after he left the islands. A local Protestant minister had written a nasty attack on the character of Father Damien, the priest who had worked with leprosy patients on Moloka'i until his death in 1889. A public letter written by Stevenson defending the late priest became widely circulated, and Father Damien soon became known and admired around the world.

Jack London, a popular author of adventure stories and novels, also wrote about the leper colony. He came to Hawai'i on his own yacht in 1907, stayed for four months, and returned a few years later for a visit that lasted nearly a year. Several of his short

While living in Hawai'i, writer Robert Louis Stevenson (right) became a friend of King Kalākaua (left).

stories used his own experiences on the islands as background material.

Somerset Maugham, a noted English author, came to the islands during World War I. He is credited with the saying that Hawai'i is the "meeting place of East and West."

The fictitious detective Charlie Chan, who has been immortalized in dozens of movies, was created by a writer named Earl Derr Biggers. Many Hawaiian residents believe that the character Chan was based on an actual Chinese-Hawaiian detective.

Fortunately for modern writers and historians, some of the early missionaries wrote excellent, accurate reports of their voyages to Hawai'i and their early years on the islands. Hiram Bingham and Laura Fish Judd were two of those who left exceptionally good accounts. Contemporary fiction writer James Michener used these and other historical writings as background material for his epic novel *Hawaii*, published in 1960.

Water-related activities are the most popular form of fun in Hawai'i.

SPORTS AND RECREATION

One sport, above all others, belongs to Hawai'i: surfing. Hawaiian travel posters, postcards, and movies have familiarized the world with the sight of an athlete standing barefoot on a piece of board and riding over crashing waves to the shore.

Surfing is considered America's oldest sport. Polynesians have enjoyed this spectacular activity since ancient times. Early visitors to the islands, from Captain Cook on, were astonished and delighted with the beauty and excitement of this sport. Expert Hawai'i surfers made it look so easy as they slided gracefully over dangerous seas. The Hawaiian term for surfing is *he'e nalu*, translated roughly as "wave sliding."

World surfing competitions are held annually in Hawai'i. Sailing and paddling outrigger canoes is another traditional sport of the Pacific region that is kept alive in the Hawaiian Islands.

The collegiate Hula Bowl is held every year at Aloha Stadium in Honolulu.

Water sports far outweigh all other kinds of recreation in this island state. Residents and visitors alike go all out for swimming, snorkeling, boating, canoeing, and fishing.

Hawaiians share the interests of mainlanders in traditional American sports. Baseball, football, and basketball are all played in Hawai'i's high schools and colleges. The University of Hawai'i competes in the Western Athletic Conference of collegiate sports. The annual Pro Bowl game of the National Football League is played every year at Aloha Stadium in Honolulu.

Hawai'i has ample facilities for tennis, golf, and horseback riding. During most winters, Mauna Kea, on the Big Island, has enough snow for downhill skiing from January through March.

Biking and hiking are popular activities with tourists. There is plenty of open space for getting close to nature, and the scenery is outstanding everywhere.

On Maui, many visitors make arrangements with a local company to be taken to the edge of the Haleakalā Crater early in the morning to watch the sunrise. The company furnishes special outerwear—the early mornings are very cold at the 9,300-foot (2,835-meter) elevation—and bicycles. After watching the sunrise, the bikers take a leisurely ride down the mountain to sea level.

Chapter 9
HAWAI'I'S HIGHLIGHTS

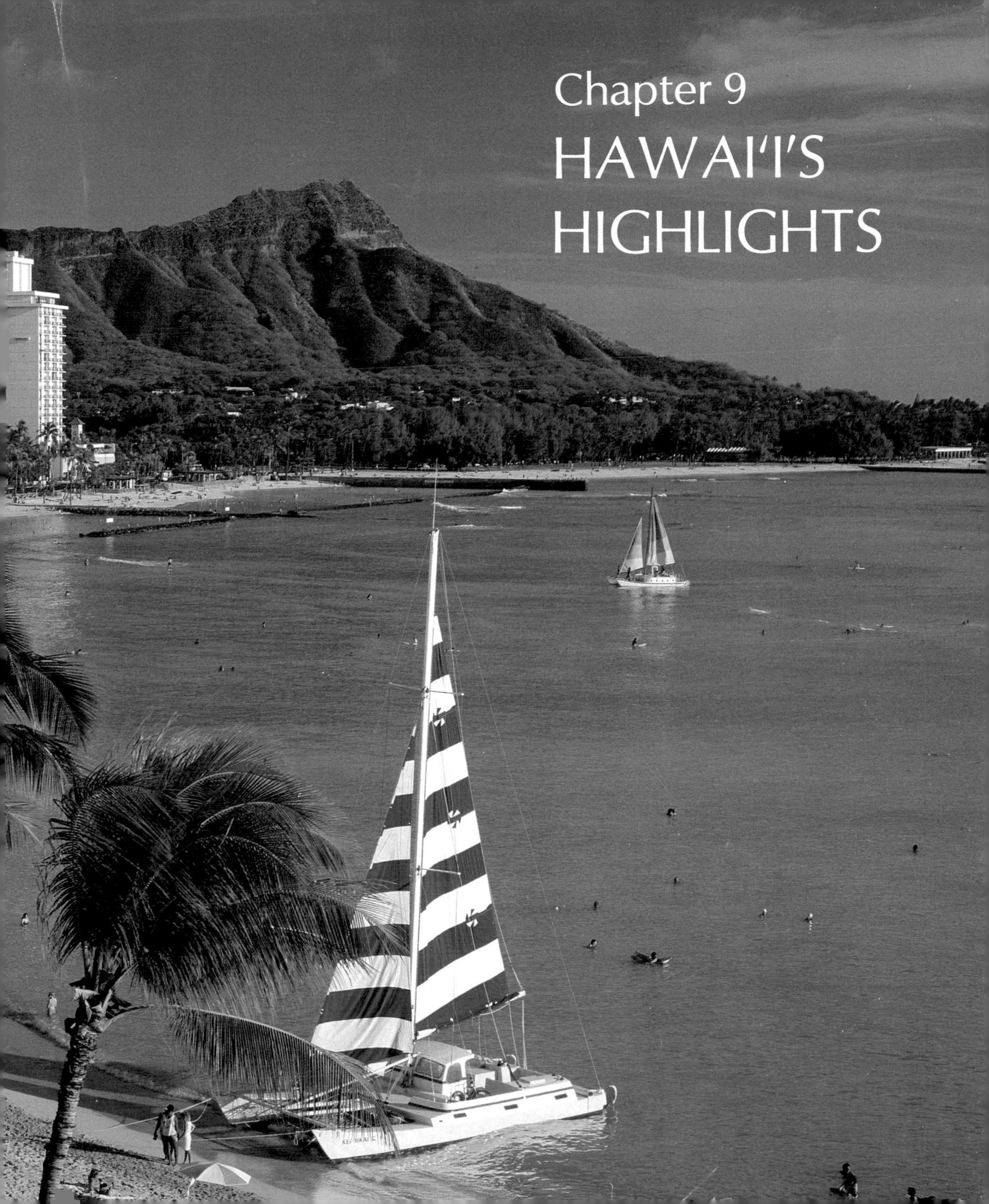

HAWAI'I'S HIGHLIGHTS

Hawai'i is beautiful from every angle: looking down toward the sea from the top of a mountain or up toward the mountains from below; flying in a plane or helicopter over volcanoes and sugarcane fields; lying on the sand and watching the changing shapes of the waves; driving through fields of tropical flowers; looking at a waterfall making its way to the ocean.

O'AHU

Most newcomers arrive first in Honolulu, the state's capital and principal city. It is a city of majestic state buildings, skyscrapers housing Hawai'i's business offices, huge resort hotels, and numerous markets, department stores, and shops filled with goods with which to lure tourists. All this, plus a splendid view of Honolulu's harbor, can be seen from an observation balcony on the tenth floor of the Aloha Tower.

People come from all over the world to visit Pearl Harbor. A white concrete memorial to the service personnel who lost their lives at Pearl Harbor on December 7, 1941, has been erected over the sunken hull of the USS *Arizona*. More than a thousand victims went down with their ship in the attack. A twenty-minute film is shown at the visitor center.

The days when Hawai'i was a kingdom are brought to life at 'Iolani Palace. Completed in 1882 during the reign of Kalākaua, it

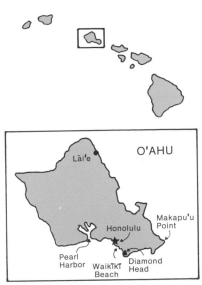

'Iolani Palace, built
by King Kalākaua in
1882, is the only royal
palace on American soil.

is the only palace in the United States where a king once held
court. The palace has been restored, and original furnishings are
gradually being recovered or replaced with facsimiles so that
visitors can experience its original splendor.

Honolulu's Bishop Museum is one of the finest museums in the
nation. It has the world's best collection of native Hawaiian and
Polynesian artifacts. The feather cloaks, helmets, and standards
once used by Hawaiian royalty are priceless. Other exhibits reflect
the experiences of the many other groups who have made Hawai'i
their home.

The Honolulu Academy of Arts is a first-class art museum and
educational center. Paintings by great European masters as well as
exquisite examples of Asian art are displayed there.

East of Honolulu's business district is Waikīkī, perhaps the world's best-known beach. Many a hardworking *kama'āina* can make it from the office to the sand and surf in just a few minutes.

The first resort on Waikīkī was the Sans Souci, built in 1884. Since then, dozens of hotels have sprung up along the beach. The strip of sand along the ocean is available to everyone, but just behind it is one of the largest concentrations of hotels anywhere, crowded together and extending away from the sea for several blocks. Jammed in among the hotels are both ultrafancy restaurants and bargain-priced carryout spots serving everything from doughnuts to fresh pineapple to Japanese tempura to gourmet croissant sandwiches. There are shops galore, a number of malls, and an international bazaar. You might have a hard time finding something as practical as a screwdriver in a Waikīkī shop, but thousands of souvenir gifts, from the ridiculous to the elegant, are everywhere to be found.

Next to the ocean at the far end of Waikīkī, away from downtown, is the state's most familiar landmark, Diamond Head. Trails lead to the top of this extinct volcano, and the view of O'ahu's south coast from the summit makes the 760-foot (232-meter) climb worthwhile.

At the foot of Diamond Head is Kapi'olani Park, an area of beaches, gardens, and picnic areas; and the Honolulu Zoo.

The easternmost tip of O'ahu is called Makapu'u Point. Sea Life Park, at Makapu'u, is one of the world's best marine parks. The park features performances of trained dolphins and whales, a whaling museum, and the Hawaiian Reef Tank, a "living re-creation" of offshore Hawai'i.

The northwest coast of O'ahu is called the Windward Side of the island. The village of Lā'ie, in this area, was settled by Mormon missionaries in the nineteenth century. Visitors to this

The Polynesian Cultural Center features demonstrations of traditional crafts and customs from seven areas of Polynesia.

mostly Mormon community may explore the beautiful grounds of the Mormon Temple, the Hawai'i campus of Brigham Young University (BYU), and the Polynesian Cultural Center.

The Polynesian Cultural Center is one of the most popular attractions in the state. Part educational center and part family-theme park, it features re-creations of ancient villages from seven areas of Polynesia—Hawai'i, Tahiti, Samoa, Fiji, Tonga, Maori New Zealand, and the Marquesas. BYU students who come from the various regions provide most of the services. They demonstrate crafts and customs and take part in pageants that feature native dancing and music.

KAUA'I

Kaua'i, north of O'ahu, is not as commercially developed as O'ahu and Maui. Nature has been relatively undisturbed on most of the island. Līhu'e, a small town, is the island's major center.

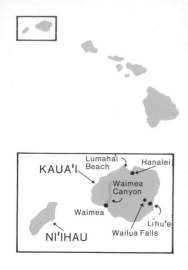

Waimea Canyon on the island of Kaua'i

Three exceptionally beautiful spots on Kaua'i are Wailua Falls, Lumaha'i Beach, and Waimea Canyon. Wailua Falls, just outside Līhu'e, was the site of ancient Hawaiian rites. Chiefs used to dive over the falls into a pool to demonstrate the courage and power given to them by the gods.

On the north side of the island, at the mouth of a fertile green valley, is Hanalei. Hanalei Bay is noted for its challenging winter surf and fine summer fishing. Lumaha'i Beach, where much of the movie *South Pacific* was filmed, lies west of the village. It is a favorite spot with photographers and people who come to watch the sunset, but it is a dangerous place for swimming.

Waimea Canyon is only a short distance west from Hanalei as the crow flies, but the steep cliffs of the Nā Pali Coast have made it impossible—or at least impractical—to build a road all around the island. So to reach the canyon by road, one must backtrack all around the island.

Waimea, the village at the southern end of the canyon, was the ancient capital of Kaua'i. It was also the site of Captain Cook's first landing on the islands. The canyon itself is a 10-mile (16-kilo-meter) series of deep, brilliantly colored gorges. They may be viewed from several lookout points.

MAUI, LĀNA'I, AND MOLOKA'I

Maui has become increasingly popular as a tourist destination in recent years. Many visitors call it their favorite island.

Maui's main airport is at Kahului, on the north side of the island at the juncture of East Maui and West Maui. Hāna, an old village rich in history and Hawaiian lore, lies a long but beautiful drive east of the airport.

Haleakalā National Park preserves a portion of wilderness land that has been considered sacred by the island's natives for more than a thousand years. Haleakalā's huge volcanic crater is Maui's most prominent natural asset.

The volcano's name, derived from the Hawaiian words *hale* (house) and *lā* (sun), means "house of the sun." It was here, Hawaiian legend says, that the demigod Māui captured the sun and made it move more slowly so that human beings could have more daylight.

Visitors to Maui are encouraged to go to the rim of the crater to watch the sun rise over its edge. Many people camp out overnight in Haleakalā National Park in order to be there at daybreak; others get up in the middle of the night to drive up to the 10,023-foot- (3,055-meter-) high crater. All of them crowd around, cameras at the ready, waiting to catch the first beams of light.

Exhibits at the park's visitor center tell of the volcano's history. The park is the home of a few rare *nēnē* (Hawaiian geese), the official state bird. Several uncommon plants grow here, including the silversword. This silvery-leaved, rosettelike plant grows in

Haleakalā Crater on the island of Maui

clumps. In some spots, large quantities of silverswords cause entire hillsides to take on a silver glow in the sunlight.

The village of Makawao, on the Haleakalā Highway, looks as if it were transplanted from Texas. Cattle ranching and diversified farming are carried out in this region. An annual rodeo is held in Makawao every July 4.

A good place to see and learn about the many different kinds of fruits, flowering plants, and other crops raised in Hawai'i is Maui's Tropical Plantation, near the Kahului Airport. Knowledgeable guides take visitors on tram rides through the orchards and gardens.

Resort hotels dot the shoreline of West Maui and the western side of East Maui. Lahaina lies on the coast of West Maui. Once known as the whaling capital of the Pacific, it was for many years a rowdy and flourishing port. It was also the capital of the islands from 1820 to 1845 and an important center of missionary activity. Today, it is Maui's most active tourist center. Boats take passengers from Lahaina on day-long cruises and fishing trips, as well as on excursions to nearby Lāna'i and other small islets.

Pineapple-growing is the predominant activity on the island of Lāna'i. Lāna'i is known as the "World's Largest Pineapple Plantation." One company, Castle & Cooke (which owns the Dole

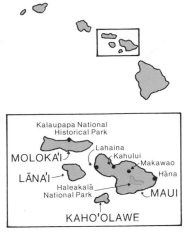

Corporation), owns 98 percent of the land. The company has allowed some tourism on the island and plans to build more hotels in the future.

The former leper colony on Moloka'i is now preserved within Kalaupapa National Historical Park. This beautiful but isolated piece of land is separated from the rest of the island by a high bluff. The only way to reach it is to fly into a tiny landing field or climb down a steep trail by foot or on muleback.

There are several hotels on Moloka'i. Near one of them is the Moloka'i Ranch Wildlife Park, a preserve inhabited by animals from Africa. Visitors can go "on safari" by van through the ranch to see giraffes, oryxes, and other exotic animals.

THE BIG ISLAND

The fire goddess Pele is said to reside on the Big Island in Kīlauea, one of the most active volcanoes on earth. Kīlauea and Mauna Loa, both part of Hawai'i Volcanoes National Park, spew out tons of new earth in the form of lava every few years.

Roads in the park circle the rim of Kīlauea's craters and the

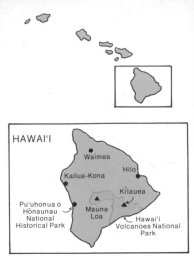

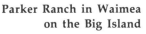

**Parker Ranch in Waimea
on the Big Island**

Kīlauea Caldera. A caldera is a huge crater caused by the collapse of earth around the spot where a volcano erupted. At the park service's two visitor centers, interesting displays illustrate aspects of Hawaiian culture.

The two major cities on the Big Island are Hilo, on the east coast; and Kailua-Kona, on the west. Each have airports that provide both interisland and international service. Hilo is the fourth-largest city in the state. It is primarily a business center, not a resort city. Several nearby scenic areas feature caves, waterfalls, and gardens.

Parker Ranch, in the northern part of the island, is the largest privately owned ranch in America. Some fifty thousand head of cattle graze on nearly a quarter-million acres (about a hundred thousand hectares) of pastureland there. The town of Waimea features a museum chronicling the history of the ranch.

Kailua-Kona is a city rich in history. King Kamehameha I spent his last years there, and both the first Protestant church and first Catholic church in the islands were built there. It is also a popular tourist area noted for its fine deep-sea fishing. Several luxury hotels have been built along the coast in recent years.

South of Kailua-Kona is Puʻuhonua o Hōnaunau National

Hulihe'e Palace, in Kailua-Kona on the Big Island, once served as a summer residence for Hawaiian royalty.

Historical Park. It is the site of a *pu'uhonua*, or place of refuge, that was built in the fifteenth century. In those times, if a person who had broken *kapu* laws managed to reach a *pu'uhonua* without being caught by pursuing warriors, he was allowed to live there in peace for the rest of his life. Park-service workers explain the history of the sanctuary and demonstrate ancient crafts.

And here, in this benevolent spot, we leave this fascinating island state. Hawai'i, so different from the other forty-nine, yet so American, has much to teach the rest of the nation. Its history, its location and geography, its geology, and its mixture of people are all worth learning about because they are a part of the wonderful diversity that is the United States.

FACTS AT A GLANCE

GENERAL INFORMATION

Statehood: August 21, 1959, fiftieth state

Origin of Name: According to one ancient Hawaiian legend, the islands were named in honor of the legendary Polynesian chief Hawai'i-loa, who is said to have been the discoverer of the islands. Another explanation is that the early Polynesian settlers named the islands after their far-off South Pacific homeland, which in ancient times had been called *Hawaiki*.

State Capital: Honolulu, on the island of O'ahu

State Nickname: The Aloha State

State Flag: The state flag features eight horizontal stripes of red, white, and blue; and a Union Jack in the upper left-hand corner. The eight stripes represent the eight main islands of Hawai'i; the Union Jack is a reminder of England's role in Hawai'i's history.

State Motto: *Ua mau ke ea o ka 'āina i ka pono*, Hawaiian words meaning "The life of the land is perpetuated in righteousness"

State Bird: *Nēnē* (Hawaiian goose)

State Flower: Hibiscus

State Tree: *Kukui*

Island Emblems: Each island has its own official color and emblem:

Island	Color	Emblem
Hawai'i	red	red *lehua* blossom
Kaho'olawe	gray	*hinahina* (threadlike moss)
Maui	pink	*lokelani* flower
Lāna'i	yellow	*kauna'oa* (air plant)
Moloka'i	green	white *kukui* blossom
O'ahu	yellow	*'ilima* flower
Kaua'i	purple	*mokihana* (green berry)
Ni'ihau	white	white *pūpū* shell

State Song: "Hawai'i Pono'ī" (Our Own Hawai'i), words by King Kalākaua, music by Heinrich Berger

Hawai'i pono'ī,	Hawai'i's own,
Nānā i kou mō'ī,	Look to your king,
Ka lani ali'i,	The royal chief,
Ke ali'i.	The chief.
Chorus:	*Chorus:*
Makua lani e,	Royal father,
Kamehameha e,	Kamehameha,
Nā kāua e pale	We shall defend
Me ka ihe,	With spears.
Hawai'i pono'ī,	Hawai'i's own,
Nānā i nā ali'i,	Look to your chiefs,
Nā pua muli kou,	The children after you,
Nā pōki'i.	The young.
Hawai'i pono'ī,	Hawai'i's own,
E ka lāhui e,	O nation,
'O kāu hana nui	Your great duty
E ui e.	Strive.

POPULATION

Population: 964,691, thirty-ninth among the states (1980 census)

Population Density: 149 people per sq. mi. (58 people per km²)

Population Distribution: Approximately four-fifths of the state's population live on O'ahu, half of those in Honolulu. Only about 13 percent of Hawai'i's people live in rural areas.

Honolulu (O'ahu)	365,048
Pearl City (O'ahu)	42,575
Kailua (O'ahu)	35,812
Hilo (Hawai'i)	35,269
'Aiea (O'ahu)	32,879
Kāne'ohe (O'ahu)	29,919
Waipahu (O'ahu)	29,139
Mililani Town (O'ahu)	21,365
Schofield Barracks (O'ahu)	18,851

Population Growth: Early population figures for Hawai'i are only estimates, as the Hawaiian government did not begin taking a census until 1850. The first U.S. government census of Hawai'i occurred in 1900. Two interesting facts about changes in the islands' population should be noted. First, the population declined

A Maui fruit vendor

drastically during the century following Captain Cook's discovery of the islands, because so many native Hawaiians died of diseases brought by foreigners. Second, during World War II, Hawai'i's population more than doubled because of the large numbers of armed forces stationed there.

Year	Population
1778	250,000-300,000
1850	84,165
1860	69,800
1872	56,897
1884	80,578
1890	89,990
1900	154,001
1910	191,874
1920	255,881
1930	368,300
1940	422,770
1944	858,945
1950	499,794
1960	632,772
1970	769,913
1980	964,691

GEOGRAPHY

Borders: The state of Hawai'i is an archipelago (chain) of islands in the North Pacific Ocean about 2,390 mi. (3,846 km) southwest of California. The entire chain, which includes 132 islands, stretches 1,523 mi. (2,451 km) from southeast to northwest. Most of the islands are small and unpopulated. Eight main islands lie in

111

The Wailuku River on the Big Island

the southeast part of the chain: Kauaʻi, Niʻihau, Oʻahu, Molokaʻi, Lānaʻi, Maui, Kahoʻolawe, and Hawaiʻi. Hawaiʻi is the nation's southernmost state and the only state that is not part of the North American mainland.

Highest Point: Mauna Kea, on the island of Hawaiʻi, 13,796 ft. (4,205 m) above sea level

Lowest Point: Sea level, along the coasts of all the islands

Area: 6,471 sq. mi. (16,760 km²)

Rank in Area Among the States: Forty-seventh

Rivers: Because of its volcanic terrain, Hawaiʻi has few rivers. The only major river is Wailuku River on Hawaiʻi Island.

Lakes: The largest natural lake is 182-acre (74-hectare) Lake Hālāliʻi, on Niʻihau. The state's largest artificial lake is Wahiawā Reservoir, which spreads over 422 acres (171 hectares) on Oʻahu.

Topography: The Hawaiian Islands are actually the top of a large, partially submerged mountain range. They have been formed by volcanic activity and consist of lava rock and coral reefs partially covered over with thin layers of soil and sand. Some scientists believe that a new Hawaiian island formed by an existing undersea volcano may emerge some day. The land of the islands is constantly being eroded by tropical rainfalls and the battering of the Pacific Ocean. The interiors of

Sunset from the peak of Mauna Kea

all the islands are mountainous. Many of the mountains are cut by huge canyons. Rugged cliffs mark some areas of the shorelines; others have broad, white or black sand beaches.

Climate: Hawai'i's climate is temperate even though the islands lie in the earth's tropical zone. The temperature is moderated by ocean breezes from the northeast and rarely climbs very high. The highest recorded temperature, 100° F. (38° C), occurred at Pāhala on April 27, 1931. Because the Hawaiian Islands lie close to the equator, days and nights are of almost equal length throughout the year, and there is little variation in temperature from one season to another. In the lowlands, the temperature stays between 70° and 85° F. (21° and 29° C) throughout the year. Cooling rains keep the air moist and pleasant. The weather does get cold high in the mountains; most winters, there is enough snow on top of Mauna Kea to allow skiing. Hawai'i's all-time low temperature, 14° F. (-10° C), was recorded at Haleakalā Crater on January 2, 1961.

NATURE

Trees and shrubs: Because of Hawai'i's isolation in the vast Pacific Ocean, the islands once had an unusually large number of plants found nowhere else in the world. Unfortunately, 38 percent of these native plants are now extinct or endangered. Hawai'i also has indigenous plants, such as many beach plants, that can be found in other parts of the world. Many of the trees and shrubs seen growing today are introduced, rather than native, plants. The taro, koa, breadfruit, bamboo, and banana plants are among those that were brought by the early Polynesians because of their usefulness. A great many of the flowering and fruit trees and shrubs that give Hawai'i its luxuriant appearance were introduced to the islands in the 1800s. These include coconut, mango, papaya, guava, and avocado trees; such shrubs as bougainvillea, oleander, and hibiscus; and the pineapple plant. Other introduced species include evergreens, eucalyptuses, Norfolk pines, banyans, and monkeypods.

Hawai'i is home to such exotic plants as
(clockwise from top left) bird of paradise,
silversword, protea, and bougainvillea.

Wildflowers: Although hundreds of species of orchids are grown commercially
in Hawai'i, only four of these are native. A few native species of wildflowers and
wild plants persist in the mountains above 1,500 ft. (457 m); below that, virtually
all native plants have been replaced by species introduced by man.

Animals: Scientists believe that the hoary bat and the monk seal were the only
mammals living on the islands before settlers arrived. They are very rarely seen by
residents. Marine mammals such as whales and dolphins have lived in Hawaiian
waters since ancient times. Domestic animals were introduced by the Polynesians
and Europeans. Today, deer, wild boars, wild goats and sheep, rats, frogs, toads,
and mongooses are among the few kinds of animals found in the wild in Hawai'i.

Birds: The Hawaiian Islands are inhabited by several rare species found nowhere
else in the world. These include the *nēnē* (Hawaiian goose), the Hawaiian stilt, and

Hawai'i's many colorful species of fish are a delight to scuba divers and snorkelers.

several species of Hawaiian honeycreepers. Other species include Hawaiian ducks, Laysan ducks, gallinules, coots, Hawaiian hawks, Hawaiian crows, short-eared owls, Nihoa millerbirds, Hawaiian thrushes, Kaua'i thrushes, black-crowned night herons, petrels, mynas, sparrows, cardinals, doves, puffins, Laysan finches, Nihoa finches, pheasants, quail, and Old World warblers. Small golden plovers from Alaska and ducks from various parts of the North American mainland migrate to Hawai'i for the winter.

Fish: About seven hundred species of fish swim in Hawaiian waters, including yellowfin tuna, *mahimahi* (dolphin), marlin, *ulua* (Jack Crevalle), wahoo, bass, big eye, goat fish, squirrel fish, parrot fish, and red fish. Young silver perch, *manini* (reef surgeonfish), blennies, and damselfish can be found in tidal pools.

GOVERNMENT

Hawai'i's constitution was adopted by the citizens of the Territory of Hawai'i in 1950 and amended by the statehood plebiscite of 1959. There are three branches of government: executive, legislative, and judicial.

The executive branch is headed by a governor and lieutenant governor who are elected to four-year terms. The governor may serve only two terms. The governor appoints, with the approval of the senate, the heads of the state's seventeen executive departments. The governor can veto legislation, but vetoes can be overridden by a two-thirds vote of the legislature.

Hawai'i's bicameral (two-house) legislature has twenty-five senators and fifty-one representatives. State senators are elected for four-year terms; state representatives serve two-year terms. General sessions of the legislature begin in January and last for sixty days.

The judicial branch of state government consists of a state supreme court, four circuit courts, and twenty-seven district courts. The supreme court has a chief justice and four associate justices. Supreme-court justices are appointed by the governor, with the approval of the senate, for ten-year terms. Circuit-court judges are also appointed by the governor for ten-year terms.

Hawai'i is unique among the states in that it has only two levels of government: state and county. Hawai'i's cities are governed and administered by the county to which they belong. There are no separate, self-governing municipalities and no local school districts in the state.

Number of Counties: 5

U.S. Representatives: 2

Electoral Votes: 4

Voting Qualifications: Eighteen years of age

EDUCATION

Hawai'i's public school system was founded in 1840. Hawai'i is the only state in which one board of education administers one public school system for the entire state.

The Kamehameha Schools are an important private educational institution. When a wealthy and prominent Hawaiian woman named Bernice Pauahi Bishop died in 1884, she left behind a sizable estate. Her wish was that the income generated by the estate would be used for the founding and endowment of schools for native Hawaiian children. Today, the Bishop Estate—whose funds can be used only to support and improve the Kamehameha Schools—is worth more than $2.3 billion. More than three thousand students of Hawaiian ancestry attend these fine elementary and secondary schools. Another thirty-five thousand young people are served through outreach programs.

About 75 percent of Hawai'i's residents who are twenty-five years of age or older have completed high school, and 20 percent have had at least four years of college.

The University of Hawaii has three campuses: Mānoa (in Honolulu), Hilo, and West O'ahu. The state has six community colleges and four private colleges. Brigham Young University-Hawai'i Campus, at Lā'ie on O'ahu, is affiliated with the Mormon church. Chaminade University of Honolulu was founded by the Marianist Fathers. Hawaii Loa College at Kāne'ohe on O'ahu and Hawaii Pacific College in Honolulu are small, independent, liberal-arts colleges.

ECONOMY AND INDUSTRY

Principal Products:
Agriculture: Sugarcane, pineapples, orchids and anthuriums, Norfolk pine trees, beef cattle, poultry, hogs, macadamia nuts, coffee, tropical fruits, vegetables, prawns

Sugarcane fields on the island of Kaua'i

Manufacturing: Food processing (sugar, pineapples, pineapple juice and concentrate), printed materials, textiles and apparel, concrete, chemicals, fabricated metal products, electronics

Natural Resources: titanium oxide (a pigment used in paint), stone, sand, gravel, pumice, yellowfin tuna, skipjack tuna

Business and Trade: Tourism and government services are the major sources of income in Hawai'i. The federal government is the largest single employer in the islands.

Communication: Nine daily newspapers are published in Hawai'i: six in English, one in both Japanese and English, one in Korean, and one in Chinese. There are twenty-seven AM radio stations, twenty FM stations, and sixteen television stations, as well as ten cable television companies. The University of Hawaii Press is an active book publisher, and about sixty magazines and other periodicals are published in the state. Several smaller book publishers also make their headquarters in Hawai'i.

Transportation: The 6-mi. (9.6-km) Lahaina-Kā'anapali & Pacific Railroad line, which takes tourists through sugarcane fields in Maui, is the only operating railroad in the state. Public bus systems operate on O'ahu and the Big Island. Two-thirds of the state's 4,300 mi. (6,920 km) of public highways are on O'ahu and the Big Island. The state has seven deep-water ports. Air travel is the most common form of transportation among the islands and between Hawai'i and other parts of the world. Hawai'i is served by more than fifty airports. The largest is Honolulu International Airport, one of the nation's busiest airports.

The Bishop Museum in Honolulu houses the world's finest collection of Hawaiian and Polynesian artifacts.

SOCIAL AND CULTURAL LIFE

Museums: Hawai'i has forty-five major museums and cultural attractions that together draw more than 12 million visitors a year. On O'ahu, among the most popular are the Polynesian Cultural Center in Lā'ie, which features re-creations of ancient villages from seven areas of Polynesia; the Bishop Museum, a world-renowned museum that specializes in Polynesian cultural and natural history; and the Honolulu Academy of the Arts, which has a fine collection of European, Asian, and Hawaiian art. The Mission Houses Museum in Honolulu is a complex of three of the earliest American buildings in Hawai'i. The Lyman House Memorial Museum in Hilo on the Big Island was built in 1839 as a residence for missionary David Lyman and his wife. It is now an excellent museum illustrating Hawai'i's ancient culture and natural history. Kamuela Museum in Waimea on the Big Island features a large collection of ancient Hawaiian tools, some possessions of Queen Lili'uokalani, and original furniture brought to Hawai'i by the early missionaries. Other noteworthy museums include the Kaua'i Museum and Creative Arts Center in Līhu'e on Kaua'i; and, on Maui, the Maui Historical Society Museum in Wailuku and the Baldwin Home Missionary Museum in Lahaina.

Libraries: Hawai'i's forty-seven public libraries are all part of the state library system. Extensive collections of materials about Hawai'i and the Pacific can be found in Honolulu at the Hawai'i State Library, the Hamilton Library of the University of Hawai'i, the Hawaiian Historical Society Library, and the Bishop Museum. The East-West Center is rich in resources on Asian affairs.

The Royal Hawaiian Band, shown here marching in the Aloha Week Parade, was organized in 1870.

Performing Arts: The Honolulu Symphony Orchestra gives regular concerts on both O'ahu and the neighboring islands. Hawaii Opera Theater presents three performances each season. There are three major theater companies on O'ahu—Honolulu Community Theater, Honolulu Theater for Youth, and Windward Theater Guild.

In 1868, at the request of King Kamehameha V, a musician named Heinrich Berger came from Germany to organize a royal band. Berger, who directed the Royal Hawaiian Band from 1872 to 1915, is today known as the Father of Hawaiian Music. He arranged more than a thousand traditional Hawaiian songs and composed many new ones. The Royal Hawaiian Band still exists, giving several concerts a week.

Hollywood movies of the 1930s did much to popularize native Hawaiian music and dance, and Hawaiian music enjoyed a "golden age" until the late 1950s. Recently, as Hawaiians have begun to rediscover their heritage, traditional Hawaiian arts have enjoyed a rebirth, and professional musicians and dancers perform regularly in many public places.

Sports and Recreation: The National Football League's annual Pro Bowl game and the collegiate Hula and Aloha bowls are played in Aloha Stadium in Honolulu. Hawai'i also hosts professional competitions in such sports as golf, surfing, triathlon, yacht racing, and game fishing. Popular high-school and college sports are baseball, football, and basketball.

Hawai'i's year-round mild weather, beautiful terrain, and spectacular coastal areas offer unparalleled opportunities for hiking, swimming, running, boating, surfing, scuba diving, snorkeling, and deep-sea fishing.

Historic Sites and Landmarks:

Alakoko Fishpond, near Līhu'e on Kaua'i, is said to have been built by the *menehune,* a legendary, ancient race of little people who were supposedly the first to inhabit Kaua'i.

Pu'uhonua o Hōnaunau National Historical Park

Hulihe'e Palace, in Kailua-Kona on Hawai'i, was built in 1838 as a summer residence for Hawaiian royalty. Furniture and other possessions of the kings and queens are on display.

'Iolani Palace, in Honolulu on O'ahu, is a magnificent building that was the official residence and royal court of Hawai'i's last two monarchs.

Kalaupapa National Historical Site, on Kalaupapa Peninsula on Moloka'i, is the site of the isolated settlement where Father Damien helped victims of Hansen's disease. The disease was virtually conquered through new drugs introduced in the 1940s, and the entire peninsula was turned over to the National Park Service in 1980.

Kawaiaha'o Church, in Honolulu on O'ahu, is the oldest church in Honolulu. Built in 1841, it served for a number of years as the royal chapel of the Hawaiian monarchs. King Lunalilo is buried in its courtyard. Its Sunday morning services are held in both English and Hawaiian.

Lapakahi State Historical Park, near Kawaihae on Hawai'i, is a partial restoration of an ancient Hawaiian fishing village.

Moku'aikaua Church, in Kailua-Kona on Hawai'i, was the first Christian church built in the islands. Completed in 1827, it was erected, with the help of native

The National Memorial Cemetery of the Pacific

Hawaiians, by the Protestant New England missionaries who had come to Hawai'i in 1820.

National Memorial Cemetery of the Pacific, in Honolulu on O'ahu, is located at Puowaina (Punchbowl), the crater of an extinct volcano. Buried here are more than twenty-one thousand Americans who were killed in World War II, the Korean Conflict, and the war in Vietnam.

Pu'uhonua o Hōnaunau National Historical Park, near Hōnaunau on Hawai'i, was one of several sacred areas where people who had broken *kapu* laws could find protection. Costumed interpreters demonstrate ancient Hawaiian crafts.

Pu'ukoholā Heiau National Historic Site, in Kawaihae on Hawai'i, is the site of a temple that was ordered built by Kamehameha the Great a few years before he founded the Kingdom of Hawai'i. Completed in 1791, it was the last major Hawaiian temple built.

Queen Emma Summer Palace, in Honolulu on O'ahu, was built in 1847 as a cool summer retreat by the Hawaiian royal family. It has been restored and furnished with many possessions of Queen Emma and King Kamehameha IV.

The USS *Arizona* National Memorial was constructed directly over the sunken battleship.

 USS Arizona National Memorial, at Pearl Harbor on Oʻahu, is a poignant memorial to the 1,177 men who were killed aboard the ship USS *Arizona* during the attack on Pearl Harbor on December 7, 1941. A white steel-and-concrete memorial building has been erected in the water directly over the sunken ship.

 USS Bowfin, at Pearl Harbor on Oʻahu, is a submarine that operated in the Pacific during World War II. It is moored next to the USS *Arizona* and is maintained as a memorial to members of the "Silent Service," those who served on submarines.

 Waiʻoli Mission House, in Hanalei on Kauaʻi, was one of the first American-style houses built on the island of Kauaʻi.

Other Interesting Places to Visit:

 ʻAkaka Falls State Park, near Hilo on Hawaiʻi, is a dense, tropical jungle park with two spectacular waterfalls.

 Carthaginian II Floating Museum, in Lahaina on Maui, is an example of the type of ship that brought the first missionaries from New England to Lahaina. Exhibits and programs tell about the days of whaling and the habits of whales.

 Diamond Head State Monument, in Honolulu on Oʻahu, is a park enclosing the 760-ft. (232-m) extinct volcano known as Diamond Head. Excellent views of the city and the ocean can be seen from the volcano's rim.

Foster Botanic Gardens, in Honolulu on O'ahu, was established in 1855 by Queen Kalama, wife of Kamehameha III. Tropical trees, orchids, ferns, palms, and exotic grasses are among the four thousand kinds of plant life found here.

Haleakalā National Park, on Maui, preserves the 10,023-ft. (3,055-m) dormant volcano that dominates the eastern part of the island of Maui. Haleakalā's crater is 3,000 ft. (914 m) deep and measures 22 mi. (35 km) in circumference. Visitors are encouraged to drive to the rim of the canyon in the early morning hours to watch the sun rise over the crater.

Hawai'i Volcanoes National Park, on Hawai'i, includes two volcanoes: Mauna Loa, the world's largest volcano; and Kīlauea. Both erupt periodically, sending broad rivers of slow-moving molten lava down their slopes. Visitors can safely observe the volcanic activity.

Kaūmana Caves, near Hilo on Hawai'i, are lava tubes that were formed more than a century ago by one of Mauna Loa's eruptions.

Keōmuku, on Lāna'i, is a ghost town that was once a flourishing sugar-plantation town. It was abandoned in 1901 after the collapse of the Maunalei Sugar Company.

Lahaina-Kā'anapali & Pacific Railroad, on Maui, is a replica of a narrow-gauge railroad that was used to haul sugarcane in the 1890s. Passengers can take a 6-mi. (9.6-km) scenic ride through the sugarcane fields.

Lava Tree State Park, in Pāhoa on Hawai'i, is a group of large *ohia* trees that were engulfed by a lava flow from Kīlauea in 1790. When the molten lava drained away from the forest, the trees, encased in hardened lava shells, remained.

Makawao, on Maui, is a trade center for the nearby cattle ranch country. Cowboys gather here, especially for the popular annual July 4th rodeo.

Maui Tropical Plantation, near Kahului on Maui, is a demonstration orchard and agricultural village. Visitors can take a tram ride past groves of fruit and nut trees, flowering plants, and aquaculture ponds.

Moloka'i Ranch Wildlife Park, on Moloka'i, is an 800-acre (324-hectare) game ranch where animals from Africa and Asia roam freely in a natural setting similar to that of their native habitat.

Nani Mau Gardens, in Hilo on Hawai'i, is a place that lives up to its name. *Nani mau* means "forever beautiful." The gardens feature about two thousand varieties of orchids, acres of other flowers, a Japanese garden, and a garden of rare Hawaiian and other herbs.

Nu'uanu Pali, at the head of Nu'uanu Valley on O'ahu, is a precipice that ranks as one of the world's most spectacular scenic overlooks. From a high spot on Pali Highway the windward coast is spread out far below. Huge cliffs rise above the overlook on either side.

Exotic animals roam freely at Moloka'i Ranch Wildlife Park.

Parker Ranch Visitor Center and Museum, in Waimea on Hawai'i, has interesting displays illustrating the life of the *paniolo* (cowboy) on Hawai'i's ranches.

Polynesian Cultural Center, in Lā'ie on O'ahu, is a cluster of villages representing ancient life in Samoa, New Zealand, Fiji, Tahiti, Hawai'i, the Marquesas, and Tonga. Customs, sports, arts, and crafts of these native cultures are demonstrated and explained. Musical pageants feature ancient and authentic dances and chants.

Sea Life Park, at Makapu'u Point on O'ahu, features an aquarium displaying Hawai'i's exotic marine life, a whaling museum, a bird sanctuary, and shows with performing dolphins and whales.

Sleeping Giant, on Kaua'i, is a mountain ridge that resembles a sleeping giant.

Wailua River State Park, in Wailua on Kaua'i, is a beautiful area with beaches, mountains, a fern grotto, and a waterfall. It was once the site of a group of sacred temples.

Waimea Canyon, on Kaua'i, is a spectacular gorge sometimes referred to as the ''Grand Canyon of the Pacific.''

Waimea Falls Park, near Hale'iwa on O'ahu, is a scenic botanical garden where hula shows and cliff-diving demonstrations are presented every day.

Wai'ānapanapa State Park and Cave, in Hāna on Maui, is a popular seaside park built on an old lava flow. A big inner cave can be reached only by diving into a pool and swimming underwater.

Waipi'o Valley, on Hawai'i, is a remote valley of taro patches surrounded by lush, green cliffs. Once inaccessible, it can now be explored on guided tours.

IMPORTANT DATES

c. A.D. 300-800—First Polynesian settlers, probably from the Marquesas Islands, arrive in Hawai'i

c. 1100-1300—Second group of Polynesian settlers, probably from Tahiti, arrive in Hawai'i

1778—British Captain James Cook, the first European to discover the islands, lands at Kaua'i; he names the Hawaiian Islands the Sandwich Islands after a British earl

1786—Two British and two French trading vessels stop at the islands

1795—King Kamehameha I conquers all but two of the major islands and establishes a unified kingdom

1804—First Russian ships arrive

1810—Kaua'i and Ni'ihau become part of the Kingdom of Hawai'i

1819—King Kamehameha I dies; King Kamehameha II ascends to the throne; the *kapu* system is abolished by royal decree

1820—First Protestant missionaries from New England arrive

1827—Catholic missionaries arrive

1831—Catholic missionaries are forced to leave

1835—First foreign-run sugar plantation in Hawai'i is established on Kaua'i

1836—*Sandwich Island Gazette*, first English-language newspaper west of the Rocky Mountains, begins publication

1839—A French ship blockades Honolulu and forces the Hawaiian government to free imprisoned Catholics and grant freedom of worship to Catholics

1840—King Kamehameha III grants to the people of Hawai'i the kingdom's first constitution; it establishes a supreme court and a legislature consisting of an upper house made up of nobility and a lower house made up of elected commoners; Hawai'i's public-school system is established

1845—The kingdom's capital is moved from Lahaina, Maui, to Honolulu, O'ahu

1848—The Great *Mahele* redistributes the Hawaiian lands

1850—Native tenants whose claims are approved receive *kuleana* lands; a law is passed allowing foreigners to own Hawaiian land for the first time

1852 — The first group of Chinese indentured laborers is brought to Hawai'i to work on the plantations; a new constitution is adopted

1868 — First boatload of Japanese indentured workers arrives

1870 — The Royal Hawaiian Band is organized

1874 — King Kalākaua makes an important diplomatic visit to the U.S.

1875 — Hawai'i and the U.S. sign a reciprocity treaty in which the U.S. agrees to remove a tariff on Hawaiian sugar shipped to American markets; in exchange, the Hawaiian government agrees to give the United States exclusive rights to the use of Hawai'i's ports and harbors

1885 — Sweet pineapple plants are introduced to the islands from Jamaica

1887 — King Kalākaua gives the U.S. exclusive rights to use Pearl Harbor as a naval base

1893 — Queen Lili'uokalani is deposed by an American-led revolution instigated by the sugar planters

1894 — The independent Republic of Hawai'i is formed; Sanford B. Dole is elected president

1898 — The U.S. annexes Hawai'i

1900 — A devastating fire in the Chinatown section of Honolulu leaves seven thousand people homeless; the U.S. Congress establishes the Territory of Hawai'i; all islanders are granted U.S. citizenship

1901 — The Hawaiian Pineapple Company is organized; within twenty years, pineapples become Hawai'i's second-most-important industry and Hawai'i becomes the world's leading producer of the fruit

1902 — A trans-Pacific telegraph cable links San Francisco and Honolulu

1903 — Hawai'i's territorial legislature first petitions Congress to grant statehood

1916 — Hawai'i Volcanoes National Park, on the Big Island, is established

1922 — Hawai'i's first commercial radio station begins broadcasting

1927 — The first airplane flight from the U.S. mainland to Hawai'i is made

1929 — Interisland airline service is initiated

1941 — On December 7, Japanese military planes attack Pearl Harbor on O'ahu, an act that draws the United States into World War II

The Port of Honolulu as it appeared in 1849

1946 — President Harry S. Truman urges Congress to grant statehood to Hawai'i; the International Longshoremen's and Warehousemen's Union wins an important strike

1949 — Another strike stops dock traffic for nearly six months

1950 — In anticipation of statehood, the territorial legislature ratifies a state constitution

1952 — Hawai'i's first television station goes on the air

1955 — For the first time, the Democratic party wins control of Hawai'i's legislature

1957 — The first telephone cable between the U.S. mainland and the islands begins operation

1959 — Hawai'i becomes the fiftieth state; regular jet air service begins between Hawai'i and the U.S. mainland, cutting travel time from California in half; Ala Moana, the world's largest shopping center, opens

1960 — Haleakalā National Park on Maui is established

1968 — U.S. President Lyndon Johnson and South Vietnam President Nguyen Van Thieu hold a conference in Honolulu

1974 — George Ariyoshi, the country's first governor of Japanese ancestry, is elected

1976 — *Hokule'a* ("Star of Gladness"), a double-hulled sailing canoe, sails from Hawai'i to Tahiti on a voyage meant to recall ancient canoe contact between the two Polynesian groups

1978—Hawai'i celebrates the bicentennial of the arrival of Captain James Cook to the Hawaiian Islands

1982—Eileen R. Anderson becomes the state's first woman mayor when she is elected mayor of the City and County of Honolulu; Hurricane Iwa strikes Hawai'i, causing more than $300 million in property damage

1986—John Waihee becomes the state's first elected governor of Hawaiian ancestry

1987—Hawai'i celebrates "The Year of the Hawaiian," paying tribute to the Hawaiian people and their culture; the *Hokule'a* returns from a historic, two-year "Voyage of Rediscovery" during which, guided only by ancient navigation methods, the boat retraced routes used by the early Polynesians

IMPORTANT PEOPLE

GEORGE ARIYOSHI

HEINRICH BERGER

Edna Isabel Allyn (1861-1927), founder of free public-library service in Hawai'i; started by placing small collections of books in homes, schools, community centers, and plantations; director of the Library of Hawai'i for fourteen years

George R. Ariyoshi (1926-   ), born in Honolulu; politician; first American of Japanese descent ever elected governor of one of the United States (1974-86)

Charlotte Fowler Baldwin (1805-1873), one of the original group of missionaries who sailed from New Bedford in 1820; with her husband, started schools on the Big Island and Maui; wrote journals about their experiences

Helen Desha Beamer (1881-1952), born in Honolulu; dancer, singer, composer, hula teacher; authority on Hawaiian customs; producer of cultural programs and pageants

Martha Warren Beckwith (1871-1959), folklorist, ethnographer, teacher, author; descendant of early missionaries; grew up in Honolulu and spent her later years there, after having taught at Elmira College, Mount Holyoke, Smith, and Vassar

Heinrich Berger (1844-1929), bandmaster, arranger, composer; director of Royal Hawaiian Band (1872-1915); composed music to "Hawai'i Pono'ī"; was responsible for making Hawaiian music widely popular

Hiram Bingham (1789-1869), missionary; unofficial leader of the first group of missionaries to come to Hawai'i from New England; wrote detailed journals about his experiences; helped develop a written alphabet for the Hawaiian language

Bernice Pauahi Bishop (1831-1884), born in Honolulu; philanthropist; great-granddaughter of Kamehameha the Great; left a sizable estate to found the Kamehameha Schools for the education of native Hawaiians and their descendants

Charles Reed Bishop (1822-1915), banker, philanthropist; founder of Hawai'i's first bank; cofounder of the Kamehameha Schools; established the Bernice Pauahi Bishop Museum in his wife's memory

George Q. Cannon (1827-1901), Mormon missionary; preached Mormonism to native Hawaiians on Maui; translated *Book of Mormon* into Hawaiian

Alexander Joy Cartwright, Jr. (1820-1919), designer of rules for the game of baseball; founder of Honolulu's first volunteer fire department

Captain James Cook (1728-1779), English explorer, mariner, hydrographer; explored the Pacific and Antarctic oceans; during a scientific and geographical expedition, he and his crew became the first Europeans to visit the Hawaiian Islands

Amos Starr Cooke (1810-1871), missionary, teacher; mentor of the Hawaiian monarchs of his time; ran the Chiefs' Children School with his wife, Juliette; founder of the company Castle & Cooke Ltd.

Anna Cooke (1853-1934), wife of Charles Montague Cooke; philanthropist; with her husband, founded the Aquarium at Waikīkī and the Cooke Library at Pūnahou School; after her husband's death, established the Honolulu Academy of Arts

Charles Montague Cooke (1849-1909), son of Amos and Juliette Cooke; businessman, banker, philanthropist; president of the Bank of Hawai'i and C. Brewer and Company; one of the most successful businessmen in Hawai'i's history

Isabella Kalili Desha (1864-1949), born on Hawai'i Island; famous *kumu hula* (hula teacher); taught the traditional dances to her daughter, Helen Desha Beamer, during a period when the missionaries frowned upon such traditional customs

Walter F. Dillingham (1875-1963), born in Honolulu; member of a prominent and wealthy Hawai'i family; organized the Hawai'i Polo and Racing Association; developed the Ala Moana Shopping Center, the largest in the world at the time of its opening (1959)

James Drummond Dole (1877-1958), businessman; major developer of Hawai'i's pineapple industry; organized the Hawaiian Pineapple Company, which later became the Dole Pineapple Company

HIRAM BINGHAM

BERNICE PAUAHI BISHOP

ALEXANDER CARTWRIGHT, JR.

JAMES COOK

SANFORD DOLE

DON HO

DANIEL INOUYE

DUKE KAHANAMOKU

Sanford Ballard Dole (1844-1926), born in Honolulu; lawyer, politician; cousin of James Drummond Dole; leader of the group that seized control of the government from Queen Lili'uokalani; head of provisional government (1893-94); president of Republic of Hawai'i (1894-1900); first governor of Territory of Hawai'i (1900-03)

Sarah Pierce Emerson (1855-1938), physician; one of the first woman doctors in Hawai'i

Queen Emma (1836-1885), born in Honolulu; wife of King Kamehameha IV; leader of a group that rioted in protest when David Kalākaua was elected king

Hiram Fong (1907-   ), born in Honolulu; lawyer, politician; one of Hawai'i's first two U.S. senators (1959-77); first person of Asian ancestry to serve in the U.S. Senate

Jack Wayne Hall (1914-1971), labor organizer; head of the International Longshoremen's and Warehousemen's Union (ILWU); as leader of the ILWU, led a number of successful strikes and helped unionized labor become a powerful force in Hawai'i

Chinn Ho (1904-   ), born in Honolulu; investment banker and developer; one of the state's most successful financiers

Don Ho (1930-   ), born in Honolulu; singer, entertainer, popularizer of Hawaiian music

Daniel Ken Inouye (1924-   ), born in Honolulu; politician; member of the illustrious 100/442 Regimental Combat Team; U.S. representative (1959-63); U.S. senator (1963-   ); first American of Japanese ancestry ever elected to Congress

Gerrit P. Judd (1803-1873), medical missionary; came to the islands in 1828; entered government in 1842 as advisor to King Kamehameha II; was important power behind the throne for eleven years; served as minister of foreign affairs, then minister of the interior, and finally minister of finance

Laura Fish Judd (1804-1872), missionary, wife of Gerrit P. Judd; her writings are important historical sources about the early missionary years; kept detailed journals and wrote a book, *Honolulu: Sketches of the Life, Social, Political, and Religious, in the Hawaiian Islands from 1828 to 1861*

Ka'ahumanu (1772-1832), born in Hāna, Maui; wife of Kamehameha I; declared herself *kuhina nui* ("important minister") after the death of Kamehameha I; shared leadership duties with Kamehameha II; served as regent while King Kamehameha III was a minor (1824-32); an enthusiastic convert to Christianity, she encouraged the building of mission churches and schools

Duke Paoa Kahanamoku (1889-1968), born in Haleakalā, Maui; swimmer, surfer; won 100-yard freestyle at the 1912 and 1920 Olympic Games; held the world record for almost twenty years; known worldwide as a champion surfer

David Kalākaua (1836-1891), born in Honolulu; king of Hawai'i (1874-91); musician and patron of the arts; world traveler; commissioned the building of 'Iolani Palace; granted rights to the United States to use Pearl Harbor as a port

Kamehameha I (1758?-1819), born in Kohala, Hawai'i Island; first ruler of the Kingdom of Hawai'i; known as Kamehameha the Great; unified the islands into a kingdom, which he ruled from 1795 until his death; considered Hawai'i's greatest leader

KAMEHAMEHA I

Kamehameha II (1797-1824), born in Hilo, Hawai'i Island; also called Liholiho; son of Kamehameha I; king of Hawai'i (1819-24); overthrew the *kapu* system and permitted Christian missionaries to live and preach on the islands; died suddenly during a visit to England

Kamehameha III (1813-1854), born in Kona, Hawai'i Island; also called Kauikeaouli; brother of Kamehameha II; king of Hawai'i (1825-54); was still a child when he became king, and did not actually rule until after the death of the regent, Ka'ahumanu, in 1832; signed a declaration of rights of Hawaiian subjects (1839) and a constitution establishing a legislature (1840); secured from the U.S., Great Britain, and France recognition of Hawai'i's independence; established a court system; initiated a program of land division and private ownership

KAMEHAMEHA II

Kamehameha IV (1834-1863), born in Honolulu; also called Alexander Liholiho; nephew of Kamehameha III; king of Hawai'i (1854-63); limited the power of the American missionaries; established relations with many nations; took steps to improve Hawai'i's economy; instituted social and medical programs

Kamehameha V (1830-1872), born in Honolulu; also called Lot Kamehameha; brother of Kamehameha IV; king of Hawai'i (1863-72); drew up a constitution that strengthened the powers of the monarchy; last of the direct line of descendants of Kamehameha I

WILLIAM LUNALILO

John Kidwell (1849?-1922), British horticulturist; imported the first pineapple plants to the islands

Lydia Lili'uokalani (1838-1917), born in Honolulu; sister of David Kalākaua; first queen and last ruler of the Kingdom of Hawai'i (1891-93); fought annexation of Hawai'i by the U.S.; was deposed in a bloodless coup by a group of American and European businessmen led by Sanford Dole and Lorrin Thurston; wrote the popular Hawaiian song "Aloha 'Oe" (1898)

William C. Lunalilo (1832-1874), born in Honolulu; king of Hawai'i (1873-74); was elected to succeed Kamehameha V; worked for improvements in the kingdom's constitution and for a reciprocity treaty with the U.S.

John Phillips Marquand (1893-1960), writer; lived in Honolulu during the 1930s while writing detective novels featuring the character Mr. Moto

JOHN MARQUAND

BETTE MIDLER

PATSY MINK

FATHER DAMIEN

Spark Masayuki Matsunaga (1916-   ), born on Kaua'i; politician; as member of the illustrious 100/442 Regimental Combat Team during World War II, was awarded the Bronze Star and the Purple Heart; U.S. senator (1976-   )

Bette Midler (1945-   ), born in Honolulu; actress, singer, entertainer

Patsy Takemoto Mink (1928-   ), born in Paia, Maui; U.S. representative (1965-77)

Ellison Onizuka (1946-1986), born in Kona, Hawai'i Island; astronaut, member of the crew of the space shuttle *Challenger* during its tragic last flight

Mary Kawena Pukui (1895-1986), born in Ka'u, Hawai'i Island; translator, scholar, author; expert on Hawaiian culture; co-author of such works as the *Hawaiian-English Dictionary*, *Place Names of Hawai'i*, and *Family System in Ka'u*

William F. Quinn (1919-   ), governor of the Territory of Hawai'i (1957-59); first governor of the state of Hawai'i (1959-62)

Claus Spreckels (1828-1908), businessman; came to the U.S. from Germany in 1846; became a wealthy and powerful sugar tycoon who monopolized the sugar industry on the Pacific Coast; nickname was the "Sugar King"; developed sugar plantations in Hawai'i; gained a great deal of power as an advisor of King Kalākaua

Robert Louis Stevenson (1850-1894), Scottish writer; visited Hawai'i twice; was a friend of the Hawaiian royal family; his *Open Letter to Rev. Dr. Hyde* helped make the late Father Damien of Moloka'i famous and respected around the world

Charles Stewart (1795-1870), missionary; member of the second company of missionaries sent to Hawai'i; wrote an excellent account of his experiences that was later published

Joseph Damien de Veuster (1840-1889), Belgian priest; went to Hawai'i as a missionary (1863); volunteered to help the people at the settlement on Moloka'i set aside for Hansen's disease patients; worked alone for ten of the sixteen years he spent there; contracted and eventually died of the disease himself; after his death became known as the "Martyr of Moloka'i"

GOVERNORS

William F. Quinn	1959-62
John A. Burns	1962-74
George R. Ariyoshi	1974-86
John Waihee	1986-

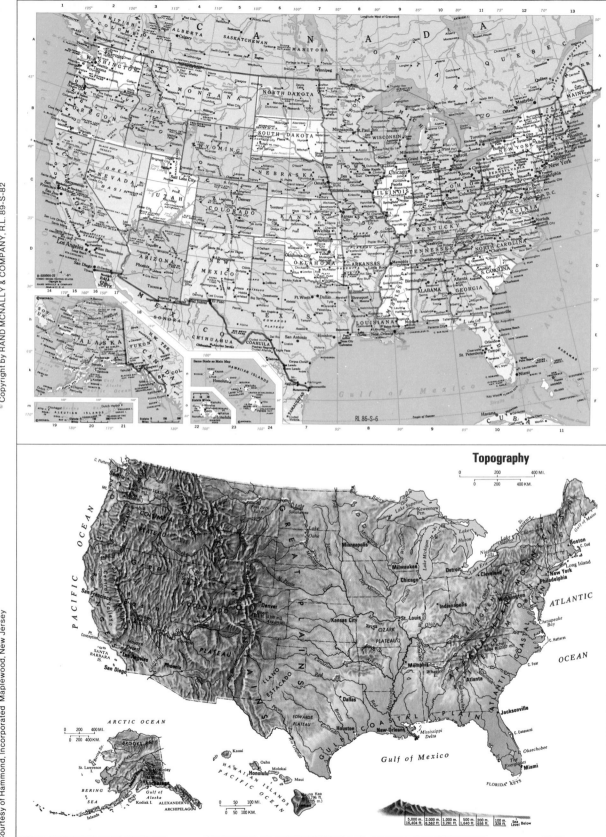

Topography

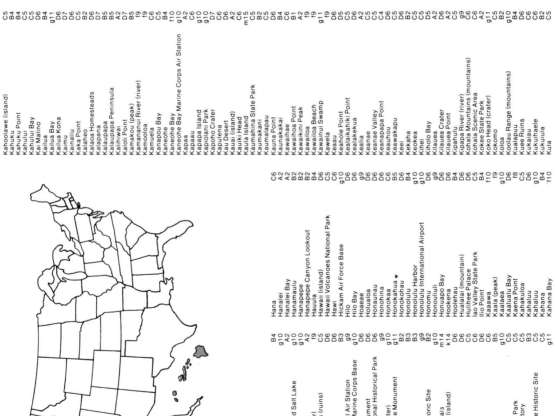

MAP KEY

Aiea B4
Ala Moana Park g10
Alakai Swamp A2
Aliamanu Crater and Salt Lake g10
Aloha Tower g10
Anahola A2
Anahulu River (river) f9
Ancient Housesites (ruins) C5
Andrade D6
Apua Point B3
Barbers Point B2
Barbers Point Naval Air Station g9
Camp H. M. Smith Marine Corps Base g10
Captain Cook D6
Captain Cook Monument D6
City of Refuge National Historical Park g9
Crestview g10
Diamond Head (crater) g11
Diamond Head State Monument g11
Eleele B2
Ewa B3
Ewa Beach g9
Ewa Beach B2
First Sugar Hill Historic Site g10
Foster Village g10
French Frigate Shoals m14
Gardner Pinnacles (island) k14
Glenwood D6
Great Lava Fissure C5
Haiku C6
Haina C6
Hakalau C6
Halaula B4
Halawa (cape) B5
Halawa Heights g10
Haleakala Crater C5
Haleakala National Park C5
Haleakala Observatory B3
Haleiwa B3
Haleki-Pihana State Historic Site C5
Haliimaile C5
Haiona Blowhole g11

Hana C6
Hanalei A2
Hanalei Bay A2
Hanamaulu B2
Hanapepe B2
Hanapepe Canyon Lookout B2
Hauula B4
Hawaii (island) D6
Hawaii Volcanoes National Park C5
Hawi C6
Hickam Air Force Base g10
Hilo D6
Hilo Bay D6
Hoaeae g9
Holualoa D6
Honaunau D6
Honohina C6
Honokaa C6
Honokahua B5
Honokohau ● B4
Honolulu g10
Honolulu Harbor B3
Honolulu International Airport g9
Honomu D6
Honouliuli g9
Honuapo Bay D6
Hookena D6
Hoolehau B4
Hualalai (mountain) D6
Hulihee Palace D6
Iao Valley State Park C5
Ilio Point B4
Kaaawa C6
Kaala (peak) f10
Kaalaea g10
Kaaluaulu Bay D6
Kaena Point B3
Kahakuloa C5
Kahaluu D6
Kahana B2
Kahana Bay B4
Kahana g11

Kahoolawe (island) C5
Kahuku B4
Kahuku Point B4
Kahului C5
Kahului Bay C5
Kai Malino B4
Kailua B4
Kailua g11
Kailua Bay B4
Kailua Kona D6
Kaimu D7
Kainaliu D6
Kaka Point C5
Kalaheo B2
Kalaoa Homesteads B4
Kalapana D7
Kalaupapa B5
Kalaupapa Peninsula B5
Kalihiwai A2
Kaloi Point D7
Kamakou (peak) B5
Kamananui River (river) f9
Kamooloa f9
Kamuela C6
Kanapou Bay A2
Kaneohe g10
Kaneohe Bay g10
Kaneohe Bay Marine Corps Air Station g10
Kapaa A2
Kapapa Island g10
Kapiolani Park g10
Kapoho Crater D7
Kapulena C6
Kauai (island) A2
Kauiki Head C6
Kaula Island A2
Kaumahina State Park m15
Kaumakani C5
Kaumalapau B2
Kauna Point C5
Kaunakakai D6
Kawaihae B4
Kawaihoa Point B2
Kawaikini Peak A2
Kawailoa f9
Kawailoa Beach f9
Kawainui Swamp g11
Kawela D6
Keaau D6
Keahole Point D6
Kealaikahiki Point C5
Kealakekua D6
Kealia D6
Keanae C5
Keanae Valley D6
Keanapapa Point B5
Keaukou C6
Keei D6
Kekaha B4
Keokea g10
Kihei D6
Kiholo Bay A2
Kilauea D6
Kilauea Crater D6
Kilauea Point D6
Kipahulu C4
Kipapa River (river) D6
Kohala Mountains (mountains) C6
Kohala Scenic Area C5
Kokee State Park A2
Koko Head (crater) f10
Kokomo C6
Koloa D6
Koolau Range (mountains) D6
Kualapuu B4
Kuee Ruins C5
Kukaiau C6
Kukuihaele B4
Kukuiula B4
Kula g11

Kumukahi (cape) C5
Kunia B4
Kure Island k12
Kurtistown D6
Laau Point B4
Lahaina B4
Laie B4
Lanai (island) g11
Lanai City D6
Lanaihale (mountain) D7
Laupahoehoe C6
Lava Tree State Park C5
Lawai B2
Laysan Island D7
Lehua (island) B5
Leleiwi Point B5
Lihue B2
Lisianski Island A2
Lower Paia C5
Lua Makika (crater) B5
Maalaea C5
Maalaea Bay C5
Maili f9
Maili Point f9
Makaha g9
Makaha Beach g9
Makaha Point g9
Makahuena Point A2
Makakilo City g9
Makapala B4
Makapuu Head g11
Makawao C5
Makaweli B2
Makena C5
Malahini Cave m15
Mamala Bay g10
Mana A2
Mana Point A2
Manana (island) g11
Maro Reef k13
Maui (island) C5
Mauna Kea (volcano) C6
Mauna Loa (volcano) D6
Maunaloa B4
Maunalua Bay g11
Maunawili g10
Menehune Gardens B2
Midway Islands k12
Mililani Town g10
Miloii D6
Moanalua Gardens g10
Moir's Cactus Garden A2
Mokapu Headland g10
Mokapu Peninsula g10
Moku Manu (island) g11
Mokuaweoweo Crater D6
Molokai (island) B4
Molokai Airport C5
Molokini (island) C5
Mountainview D6
Naalehu D6
Nanakuli D6
Napoopoo D6
National Military Cemetery of the Pacific A2
Nawiliwili Bay A2
Necker Island A2
Niihau (island) A2
Ninole C6
North Halawa River (river) C6
Numila B2
Nuuanu Pali (pass) g11
Oahu (island) B2
Olowalu B4
Ookala C5
Opaeula Camp C6
Opihikao D7
Paauhau D6
Paauilo g10
Pacific Palisades B2
Pahala C5

Pahoa D7
Paia C5
Palaoa Point C5
Palikea (mountain) g9
Paniau (peak) B1
Papaaloa D6
Papaikou D6
Papawai Point C5
Pauwela C5
Pearl City B4
Pearl Harbor D7
Pearl Harbor g10
Pearl Harbor Naval Station B4
Pepeekeo D6
Poamoho River (river) f9
Pohue Bay D6
Poipu B2
Polihale State Park B1
Pomoho C5
Prince Kuhio Birthplace C5
Pua Kaa Falls D6
Puako B1
Puea Point B2
Puhi B2
Pukalani C5
Puu Kaaumakua g9
Puu Kalena (peak) f10
Puu Keahiakahoe (peak) f10
Puu Konahuanui (peak) g9
Puu Waawaa (peak) g10
Puukohola Heiau National Historic Site C5
Puukolii g10
Puunene C5
Russian Fort State Historical Site B2
Salt Lake (lake) B2
Sand Island B5
Seven Sacred Pools C5
Sleeping Giant, scenic area A2
Spouting Horn Park B2
Spreckelsville B3
Sunset Beach B2
The Needle, rock formation B3
USS Arizona Memorial g10
Ulupalakua C5
Union Mill C6
Upolu Point C6
Volcano D6
Wahiawa g10
Wahiawa Botanical Garden g10
Wahiawa Reservoir g10
Waialua B3
Waialua Bay B3
Waianae B2
Waianapanapa Cave C5
Waianae River (river) g10
Waihee C5
Waikapu C5
Waikiki Beach g11
Wailanae (mountain range) B2
Wailau B5
Wailea C5
Wailua B2
Wailua Falls A2
Wailua River State Park A2
Wailuku C5
Wailuku River (river) C6
Waimalu C5
Waimanalo g11
Waimanalo Bay g11
Waimanalo Beach B2
Waimea B2
Waimea A2
Waimea Canyon A2
Wainiha D6
Waiohinu A2
Waipahu B3
Waipahee Falls A2
Waipio Acres g9
Waipio Peninsula g9
Wet and Dry Caves A2
Wheeler Air Force Base g9
Whitmore Village f9

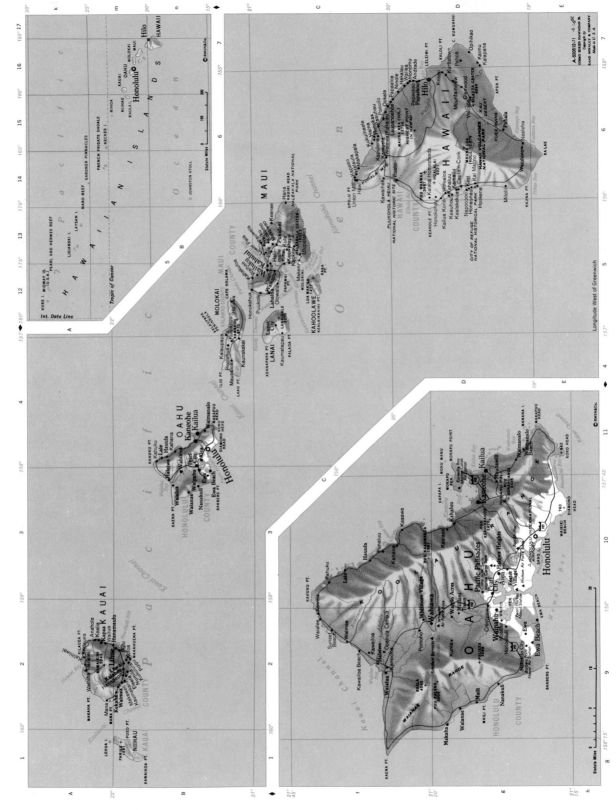

HAWAIIAN ISLANDS

Pacific Ocean

KURE I.
MIDWAY IS. (U.S.A.)
PEARL AND HERMES REEF
LISIANSKI I.
LAYSAN I.
MARO REEF
GARDNER PINNACLES
FRENCH FRIGATE SHOALS
NECKER I.
NIHOA
○ JOHNSTON ATOLL

Tropic of Cancer

Int. Date Line

NIIHAU
KAUAI
OAHU
Honolulu
MOLOKAI
MAUI
HAWAII
Hilo

Statute Miles

KAUAI

NIIHAU

OAHU
Honolulu

MOLOKAI
LANAI
KAHOOLAWE

MAUI COUNTY

MAUI

Alenuihaha Channel

HAWAII
COUNTY

HAWAII

Hilo

Honolulu

OAHU

HONOLULU COUNTY

A-500512-71 (-6 - SP
COMBO SERIES HAWAIIAN IS.
Copyright by
RAND McNALLY & COMPANY
Made in U.S.A.

Longitude West of Greenwich

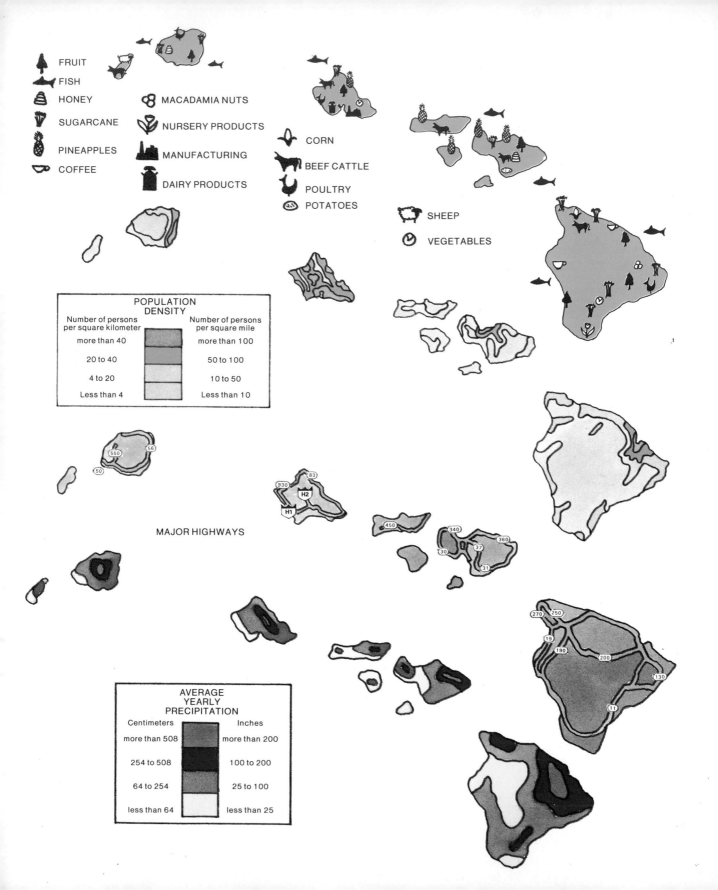

FRUIT

FISH

HONEY

SUGARCANE

PINEAPPLES

COFFEE

MACADAMIA NUTS

NURSERY PRODUCTS

MANUFACTURING

DAIRY PRODUCTS

CORN

BEEF CATTLE

POULTRY

POTATOES

SHEEP

VEGETABLES

POPULATION
DENSITY

Number of persons
per square kilometer

Number of persons
per square mile

more than 40

more than 100

20 to 40

50 to 100

4 to 20

10 to 50

Less than 4

Less than 10

MAJOR HIGHWAYS

AVERAGE
YEARLY
PRECIPITATION

Centimeters

Inches

more than 508

more than 200

254 to 508

100 to 200

64 to 254

25 to 100

less than 64

less than 25

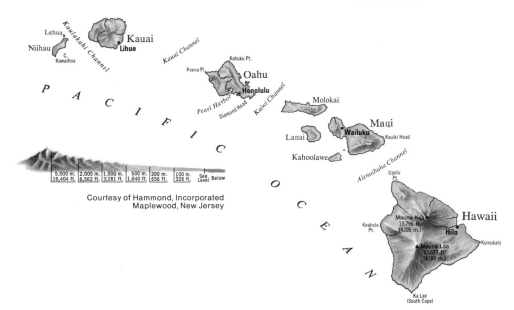

Kauai

Lehua
Niihau
C.
Kawaihoa
Kaulakahi Channel

Lihue

Kauai Channel

Kahuku Pt.
Kaena Pt.
Oahu
Honolulu
Pearl Harbor
Diamond Head

Kaiwi Channel

Molokai

Maui
Wailuku
Kauiki Head

Lanai

Kahoolawe

Alenuihaha Channel

P A C I F I C

O C E A N

Upolu
Pt.

Keahole
Pt.

Mauna Kea
13,796 ft.
(4205 m.)

Hawaii

Hilo

Kumukahi

Mauna Loa
13,677 ft.
(4169 m.)

Ka Lae
(South Cape)

| 5,000 m. | 2,000 m. | 1,000 m. | 500 m. | 200 m. | 100 m. | Sea | Below |
| 16,404 ft. | 6,562 ft. | 3,281 ft. | 1,640 ft. | 656 ft. | 328 ft. | Level | |

Courtesy of Hammond, Incorporated
Maplewood, New Jersey

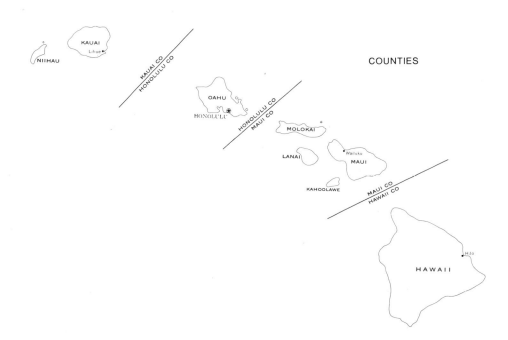

KAUAI

NIIHAU

Lihue

KAUAI CO.
HONOLULU CO.

OAHU

HONOLULU

HONOLULU CO.
MAUI CO.

MOLOKAI

LANAI

Wailuku
MAUI

KAHOOLAWE

MAUI CO.
HAWAII CO.

Hilo

HAWAII

The Nā Pali Coast of Kaua'i

INDEX

Page numbers that appear in boldface type indicate illustrations

A Hawai'i family

The Iao Needle, a famous Maui landmark

Picture Identifications

Front Cover: Hanauma Bay, O'ahu
Back Cover: An eruption of Kīlauea
Pages 2-3: Lahaina, Maui
Page 6: Prince Lot Hula Fest at Moanalua Park and Gardens, O'ahu
Pages 8-9: Kualoa Point, O'ahu
Pages 22-23: Montage of Hawai'i residents
Pages 30-31: A mural depicting Ahu'ena Heiau, where Kamehameha I spent his final years
Page 42: Statue of Kamehameha I in Honolulu
Page 62: Waikīkī Beach in 1915
Pages 76: The state capitol building with 'Iolani Palace in the background
Pages 84-85: Hawaiian surfer
Pages 96-97: Waikīkī Beach, O'ahu
Page 108: Montage showing the state flag, the state tree (*kukui*), the state flower (hibiscus), and the state bird (*nēnē*)

About the Author

Sylvia McNair is the author of numerous books for adults and young people about interesting places. A graduate of Oberlin College, she has toured all fifty of the United States and more than thirty foreign countries. Her travels have included many visits to Hawaii. Sylvia McNair lives in Evanston, Illinois. She has three sons, one daughter, and two grandsons.

Picture Acknowledgments

Front cover, © Dirk Gallian/**Journalism Services;** 2-3, **SuperStock International;** 4, © Fletcher/**H. Armstrong Roberts;** 5, © George Hunter/**TSW-Click/Chicago Ltd.;** 6, © Joe Carini/**Third Coast Stock Source;** 8-9, **SuperStock International;** 11, © P. Degginger/ **H. Armstrong Roberts;** 13, © Ed Cooper/**Shostal/SuperStock;** 15, © Joe Carini/**Third Coast Stock Source;** 16, © **Porterfield/Chickering;** 17, © Salmoiraghi/**Photo Resource Hawaii;** 18, © W. J. Scott/**H. Armstrong Roberts;** 21 (left), **SuperStock International;** 21 (right), © Vera Bradshaw/**Root Resources;** 22 (top left, bottom right), © **Cameramann International Ltd.;** 22 (bottom left), © **Joan Dunlop;** 22 (top right), **SuperStock International;** 23 (top left), © Phil Degginger/**TSW-Click/Chicago Ltd;** 23 (bottom left), © Greg Vaughn/**Tom Stack & Associates;** 23 (bottom center), © G. L. French/**H. Armstrong Roberts;** 23 (top right), © **Virginia Grimes;** 23 (right, bottom right), © Steve Lissau/**Photri;** 27, © Robert Frerck/ **Odyssey Productions;** 28 (left), © W. Bertsch/**H. Armstrong Roberts;** 28 (right), **SuperStock International;** 30-31, © Vera Bradshaw/**Root Resources;** 33, **Bishop Museum;** 34, **Bishop Museum;** 37, © Stan Goldberg Assoc. Inc./**Shostal/SuperStock;** 40, **Bishop Museum;** 41, **Bishop Museum;** 42, © Stephen Trimble/**Root Resources;** 45, **Bishop Museum;** 46 (left), **Bishop Museum;** 46 (right), © Frank Siteman/**The Marilyn Gartman Agency;** 48, **Bishop Museum;** 50, **Bishop Museum;** 51 (both pictures), **Bishop Museum;** 53, **North Wind Picture Archives;** 54, **Bishop Museum;** 55 (left), © Stan Goldberg Assoc. Inc./**Shostal/SuperStock;** 55 (right), **Bishop Museum;** 57, **Historical Pictures Service, Chicago;** 59, *Illustrated London Times;* 60 (both pictures), **Historical Pictures Service, Chicago;** 62, **Bishop Museum;** 65 (top left, top right), **Bishop Museum;** 65 (bottom), **Hawaii State Archives;** 67, **Bishop Museum;** 68, **National Archives;** 71, **Bishop Museum;** 73 (left), **AP/Wide World Photos;** 73 (right), **Bishop Museum;** 74, © S. Lissau/**H. Armstrong Roberts;** 76, © Ed Cooper/**Shostal/ SuperStock;** 79, © Robert Frerck/**Odyssey Productions;** 80, © Michael Bertan/**TSW-Click/ Chicago Ltd.;** 82 (top left), © Salmoiraghi/**Photo Resource Hawaii;** 82 (bottom left), © Phil Degginger/**TSW-Click/Chicago Ltd.;** 82 (right), © Joe Carini/**Third Coast Stock Source;** 84-85, © S. Lissau/**H. Armstrong Roberts;** 87 (left), **Bishop Museum;** 87 (right), © Bob Abraham/ **Photo Resource Hawaii;** 88, © Joe Carini/**Third Coast Stock Source;** 89 (left), © Stan Goldberg Assoc. Inc./**Shostal/SuperStock;** 89 (right), **Bishop Museum;** 90, © **Charles Jacobs;** 93, **Historical Pictures Service, Chicago;** 94 (left), © Salmoiraghi/**Photo Resource Hawaii;** 94 (right), © Dirk Gallian/**Journalism Services;** 95, © Joe Carini/**Third Coast Stock Source;** 96-97, © Reed Kaestner/**Journalism Services;** 99, © Dirk Gallian/**Journalism Services;** 99 (map), **Len W. Meents;** 101 (left), © **Bill Gleasner;** 101 (right), © **Cameramann International, Ltd.;** 102, **SuperStock International;** 102 (map), **Len W. Meents;** 104, © S. Lissau/**H. Armstrong Roberts;** 105, © Woody Mark/**Shostal/SuperStock;** 105 (map), **Len W. Meents;** 106, © Greg Vaughn/**Tom Stack & Associates;** 106 (map), **Len W. Meents;** 107, © **Porterfield/Chickering;** 108 (tree), **Photo Resource Hawaii;** 108 (flower), © **Charles Jacobs;** 108 (bird), © **Bob & Ira Spring;** 108 (flag), **Courtesy Flag Research Center, Winchester, Massachusetts 01890;** 111, © Salmoiraghi/**Photo Resource Hawaii;** 112, © D. Muench/**H. Armstrong Roberts;** 113, © George Hunter/**H. Armstrong Roberts;** 114 (top left), © Brian Parker/**Tom Stack & Associates;** 114 (bottom left), © **Virginia Grimes;** 114 (top right), © Robert Frerck/**Odyssey Productions;** 114 (bottom right), © Joe Carini/**Third Coast Stock Source;** 115 © Tom Stack/**Tom Stack & Associates;** 117, © Brian Parker/**Tom Stack & Associates;** 118, © Dirk Gallian/**Journalism Services;** 119, © **Joan Dunlop;** 120, © **Charles Jacobs;** 121, Camerique/ **H. Armstrong Roberts;** 122, © Dirk Gallian/**Journalism Services;** 124, © Salmoiraghi/**Photo Resource Hawaii;** 127, **Historical Pictures Service, Chicago;** 128 (Ariyoshi), **AP/Wide World Photos;** 128 (Berger), **Bishop Museum;** 129 (Bingham, Bishop), **Bishop Museum;** 129 (Cartwright), **The Granger Collection, New York;** 129 (Cook), **North Wind Picture Archives;** 130 (Dole), **The Granger Collection, New York;** 130 (Ho, Inouye, Kahanamoku), **AP/Wide World Photos;** 131 (Kamehameha I, Kamehameha II, Lunalilo), **The Granger Collection, New York;** 131 (Marquand), **AP/Wide World Photos;** 132 (Midler, Mink), **AP/ Wide World Photos;** 132 (Father Damien), **The Granger Collection, New York;** 136, **Len W. Meents;** 138 © Thomas Lemke/**Third Coast Stock Source;** 141, © Salmoiraghi/**Photo Resource Hawaii;** 142, © **SuperStock International**